SHAKESPEARE

OTHELLO

NOTES

COLES EDITORIAL BOARD

Bound to stay open

Publisher's Note

Otabind (Ota-bind) This book has been bound using the patented Otabind process You can open this book at any page, gently run your finger down the spine, and the pages will lie flat

ABOUT COLES NOTES

COLES NOTES have been an indispensible aid to students on five continents since 1948.

COLES NOTES are available for a wide range of individual literary works. Clear, concise explanations and insights are provided along with interesting interpretations and evaluations.

Proper use of COLES NOTES will allow the student to pay greater attention to lectures and spend less time taking notes. This will result in a broader understanding of the work being studied and will free the student for increased participation in discussions.

COLES NOTES are an invaluable aid for review and exam preparation as well as an invitation to explore different interpretive paths.

COLES NOTES are written by experts in their fields. It should be noted that any literary judgement expressed herein is just that – the judgement of one school of thought. Interpretations that diverge from, or totally disagree with any criticism may be equally valid.

COLES NOTES are designed to supplement the text and are not intended as a substitute for reading the text itself. Use of the NOTES will serve not only to clarify the work being studied, but should enhance the readers enjoyment of the topic.

ISBN 0-7740-3222-7

© COPYRIGHT 2007 AND PUBLISHED BY
COLES PUBLISHING COMPANY
TORONTO - CANADA
PRINTED IN CANADA

Manufactured by Webcom
Cover finish: Webcom's Exclusive **DURACOAT**

CONTENTS

WILLIAM SHAKESPEARE
LIFE AND WORKS

Biographical Sketch

With the epithet "Dear Son of Memory", Milton praised Shakespeare as one constantly in our memories and brother of the Muses. Certainly no other author has held such sway over the literary world, undiminished through some three and a half centuries of shifting artistic tastes. Shakespeare's plots and his characters have continued to be a living reality for us; as his well known contemporary Ben Jonson wrote, in a familiar tribute, "Thou . . . art alive still, while thy Booke doth live,/ And we have wits to read, and praise to give."

The Early Years

Despite such acclaim and the scholarship it has spawned, our knowledge of Shakespeare's life is sketchy, filled with more questions than answers, even after we prune away the misinformation accumulated over the years. He was baptized on April 26, 1564, in Holy Trinity Church, Stratford-on-Avon. As it was customary to baptize children a few days after birth, we conjecture that he was born on April 23. The monument erected in Stratford states that he died on April 23, 1616, in his fifty-third year.

William was the third child of John Shakespeare, who came to Stratford from Snitterfield before 1532 as a "whyttawer" (tanner) and glover, and Mary Arden, daughter of a wealthy "gentleman of worship" from Wilmecote. They married around 1557. Since John Shakespeare owned one house on Greenhill Street and two on Henley Street, we cannot be certain where William was born, though the Henley Street shrine draws many tourists each year. William's two older sisters died in infancy, but three brothers and two other sisters survived at least into childhood.

Shakespeare's father was fairly well-to-do, dealing in farm products and wool, and owning considerable property in Stratford. After holding a series of minor municipal offices he was elected alderman in 1565, high bailiff (roughly similar to the mayor of today) in 1568, and chief alderman in 1571. There are no records of young Will Shakespeare's education (though there are many unfounded legends), but he undoubtedly attended the town school maintained by the burgesses, which prepared its students for the universities. Ben Jonson's line about Shakespeare's having "small *Latine*, and lesse *Greeke*" refers not to his education but to his lack of indebtedness to the classical writers and dramatists.

On November 27, 1582, a licence to marry was issued to "Willelmum Shaxpere *et* Annam Whateley *de* Temple Grafton," and on

1

the next day a marriage bond for "Willm Shagspere" and "Anne Hathwey of Stratford" was signed by Fulk Sandells and John Richardson, farmers of Stratford. This bond stated that there was no "lawful let or impediment by reason of any precontract, consanguinity, affinity, or by any other lawful means whatsoever"; thus "William and Anne (were) to be married together with once asking of the banns of matrimony." The problem of Anne Whateley has led many researchers and some detractors to argue all kinds of improbabilities, such as the existence of two different Shakespeares and the forging of documents to conceal Shakespeare's true identity. The actual explanation seems to be simple: the clerk who made the marriage licence entry apparently copied the name "Whateley" from a preceding entry, as a glance at the full sheet suggests. (Incidentally, Nicholas Rowe in his life of Shakespeare, published in 1709, well before the discovery of these marriage records, gave Anne's name as Hathaway.) The problems of marriage with Anne Hathaway — he was eighteen and she was twenty-six — and of the bond have caused similar consternation. Why did these two marry when there was such a discrepancy of age? Why only one saying of the banns (rather than the usual three)? Why the emphasis on a possible legal impediment? The answer here is not simple or definite, but the birth of a daughter Susanna, baptized at Holy Trinity on May 26, 1583, seems to explain the odd circumstances. It should be recognized, however, that an engagement to marry was considered legally binding in those days (we still have breach-of-promise suits today) and that premarital relations were not unusual or frowned upon when an engagement had taken place. The circumstances already mentioned, Shakespeare's ensuing activities, and his will bequeathing to Anne "my second best bed with the furniture" have suggested to some that their marriage was not entirely happy. Their other children, the twins Hamnet and Judith, were christened on February 2, 1585.

Theatrical Life

Shakespeare's years before and immediately after the time of his marriage are not charted, but rumor has him as an apprentice to a master butcher or as a country teacher or an actor with some provincial company. He is supposed to have run away from whatever he was doing for livelihood and to have gone to London, where he soon attached himself to some theatrical group. At this time there were only two professional houses established in the London environs, The Theatre (opened in 1576) and The Curtain (opened in 1577). His first connection with the theater was reputedly as holder of horses; that is, one of the stage crew, but a most inferior assignment. Thereafter he became an actor (perhaps at this time he met Ben Jonson), a writer, and a director. Such experience had its mark in the theatricality of his plays. We do know that he was established in London by 1592, when Robert Greene lamented in *A Groatsworth of Wit* (September, 1592) that professional actors had gained priority in the theater over university-trained writers like himself: "There is an upstart Crow, beautified with our feathers, that with his *Tygers hart wrapt in a Players hyde*, supposes he is as well able to bombast out a lanke verse as the best of you: and beeing an absolute *Iohannes fac totum* (Jack-of-all-trades), is in his owne conceit the onely Shake-scene in a countrey." An apology for Greene's ill-humored statement by Henry Chettle, the editor of the pamphlet, appeared around December 1592 in *Kind-Hart's Dream*.

Family Affairs

To return to the known details of family life, Shakespeare's son Hamnet was buried at Stratford on August 11, 1596; his father was given a coat of arms on October 20, 1596; and he purchased New Place (a refurbished tourist attraction today) on May 4, 1597. The London playwright obviously had not severed connections with his birthplace, and he was reflecting his new affluence by being known as William Shakespeare of Stratford-upon-Avon, in the County of Warwick, Gentleman. His father was buried in Stratford on September 8, 1601; his mother, on September 9, 1608. His daughter Susanna married Dr. John Hall on June 5, 1607, and they had a child named Elizabeth. His other daughter, Judith, married Thomas Quiney on February 10, 1616, without special licence, during Lent and was thus excommunicated. Shakespeare revised his will on March 25, 1616, and was buried on April 25, 1616 (according to the parish register). A monument by Gerard Janssen was erected in the Holy Trinity chancel in 1623 but many, like Milton several years later, protested:

> What needs my *Shakespeare* for his honour'd Bones,
> The labour of an age in piled Stone, . . .
> Thou in our wonder and astonishment
> Hast built thy self a live-long Monument.

Shakespeare's Writings

Order of Appearance

Dating of Shakespeare's early plays, while based on inconclusive evidence, has tended to hover around the early 1590's. Almost certainly it is his chronicles of Henry the Sixth that Philip Henslowe, an important theatrical manager of the day, referred to in his diary as being performed during March-May 1592. An allusion to these plays also occurs in Thomas Nashe's *Piers Penniless His Supplication to the Devil* (August, 1592). Greene's quotation about a tiger is a paraphrase of "O tiger's heart wrapt in a woman's hide" from *Henry VI*, Part III.

The first published work to come from Shakespeare's hand was *Venus and Adonis* (1593), a long stanzaic poem, dedicated to Henry

Wriothesley, Earl of Southampton. A year later *The Rape of Lucrece* appeared, also dedicated to Southampton. Perhaps poetry was pursued during these years because the London theaters were closed as a result of a virulent siege of plague. The *Sonnets*, published in 1609, may owe something to Southampton, who had become Shakespeare's patron. Perhaps some were written as early as the first few years of the 1590's. They were mentioned (along with a number of plays) in 1598 by Francis Meres in his *Palladis Tamia*, and sonnets 138 and 144 were printed without authority by William Jaggard in *The Passionate Pilgrim* (1599).

There is a record of a performance of *A Comedy of Errors* at Gray's Inn (one of the law colleges) on December 28, 1594, and, during early 1595, Shakespeare was paid, along with the famous actors Richard Burbage and William Kempe, for performances before the Queen by the Lord Chamberlain's Men, a theatrical company formed the year before. The company founded the Globe Theatre on the south side of the Thames in 1599 and became the King's Men when James ascended the throne. Records show frequent payments to the company through its general manager John Heminge. From 1595 through 1614 there are numerous references to real estate transactions and other legal matters, to many performances, and to various publications connected with Shakespeare.

Order of Publication

The first plays to be printed were *Titus Andronicus* around February, 1594, and the garbled versions of *Henry VI*, Parts II and III in 1594. (Some scholars, however, question whether the last two are versions of *Henry VI*, Parts II and III, and some dispute Shakespeare's authorship.) Thereafter *Richard III* appeared in 1597 and 1598; *Richard II*, in 1597 and twice in 1598; *Romeo and Juliet*, in 1597 (a pirated edition) and 1599, and many others. Some of the plays appear in individual editions, with or without Shakespeare's name on the title page,but eighteen are known only from their appearance in the first collected volume (the so-called First Folio) of 1623. The editors were Heminge and Henry Condell, another member of Shakespeare's company. *Pericles* was omitted from the First Folio although it had appeared in 1609, 1611, and 1619; it was added to the Third Folio in 1664.

There was reluctance to publish plays at this time for various reasons; many plays were carelessly written for fast production; collaboration was frequent; plays were not really considered *reading* matter; they were sometimes circulated in manuscript; and the theatrical company, not the author, owned the rights. Those plays given individual publication appeared in a quarto, so named from the size of the page. A single sheet of paper was folded twice to make four leaves (thus *quarto*) or eight pages; these four leaves constitute one signature (one section of a bound book). A page measures about 6¾ in. x 8½ in. On the other hand, a folio sheet is folded once to make two leaves or four pages; three sheets, or twelve pages, constitute a signature. The page is approximately 8½ in. x 13⅜ in.

Authorized publication occurred when a company disbanded, when money was needed but rights were to be retained, when a play failed or ran into licensing difficulties (thus, hopefully, the printed work would justify the play against the criticism), or when a play had been pirated. Authorized editions are called good quartos. Piratical publication might occur when the manuscript of a play had circulated privately, when a member of a company desired money for himself, or when a stenographer or memorizer took the play down in the theater (such a version was recognizable by inclusion of stage directions derived from an eyewitness, by garbled sections, etc.). Pirated editions are called bad quartos; there are at least five bad quartos of Shakespeare's plays.

Authenticity of Works

Usually thirty-seven plays are printed in modern collections of Shakespeare's works but some recent scholars have urged the addition of two more: *Edward III* and *Two Noble Kinsmen*. A case has also been advanced, unconvincingly, for a fragment of the play on Sir Thomas More. At times, six of the generally-accepted plays have been questioned: *Henry VI*, Parts I, II and III, *Timon of Athens*, *Pericles* and *Henry VIII*. The first four are usually accepted today (one hopes all question concerning *Timon* has finally ended), but if Shakespeare did not write these plays in their entirety, he certainly wrote parts of them. Of course, collaboration in those days was commonplace. Aside from the two long narrative poems already mentioned and the sonnets (Nos. 1-152, but not Nos. 153-154), Shakespeare's poetic output is uncertain. *The Passionate Pilgrim* (1599) contains only five authenticated poems (two sonnets and three verses from *Love's Labour's Lost*); *The Phoenix and the Turtle* (1601) may be his, but the authenticity of *A Lover's Complaint* (appended to the sonnets) is highly questionable.

Who Was Shakespeare?

At this point we might mention a problem that has plagued Shakespeare study for over a century: who was Shakespeare? Those who would like to make the author of the plays someone else — Francis Bacon or the Earl of Oxford or even Christopher Marlowe (dead long before most of the plays were written) — have used the lack of information of Shakespeare's early years and the confusion in the evidence we have been examining to advance their candidate. But the major arguments against Shakespeare show the source of these speculators' disbelief to be in classconscious snobbery and perhaps in a perverse adherence to minority opinion. The most common argument is that no one of Shakespeare's background, lack of education, and lack of aristocratic experience could know all that the author knew. But study will reveal that such information was readily available in various popular sources, that some of it lies in the literary sources used for the play, and that Shakespeare was probably not totally lacking in education or in social decorum. The more significant question of style and tone is not dealt with — nor could it successfully be raised. Bacon, for example, no matter how much we admire his mind and his writings, exhibits a writing style diametrically opposite to Shakespeare's, a style most unpoetic and often flat. The student would be wise not to waste time rehashing these unfounded theories. No such question was raised in the seventeenth or eighteenth centuries, and no serious student of the plays today doubts that Shakespeare *was* Shakespeare.

Shakespeare's Plays

Exact dates for Shakespeare's plays remain a source of debate among scholars. The following serve only as a general frame of reference.

	COMEDIES	TRAGEDIES	HISTORIES
1591			Henry VI, Part I
1592	Comedy of Errors		Henry VI, Part II
1592	Two Gentlemen of Verona		Henry VI, Part III
1593	Love's Labour's Lost	Titus Andronicus	Richard III
1594			King John
1595	Midsummer Night's Dream	Romeo and Juliet	Richard II
1596	Merchant of Venice		
1596	Taming of the Shrew		
1597			Henry IV, Part I
1598	Much Ado About Nothing		Henry IV, Part II
1599	As You Like It	Julius Caesar	
1599	Merry Wives of Windsor		Henry V
1601	Twelfth Night	Hamlet	
1602	Troilus and Cressida		
1602	All's Well That Ends Well		
1604	Measure for Measure	Othello	
1605		King Lear	
1606		Macbeth	
1607		Timon of Athens	
1607		Antony and Cleopatra	
1608	Pericles		
1609		Coriolanus	
1610	Cymbeline		
1611	Winter's Tale		
1611	Tempest		
1613			Henry VIII

Shakespeare's England

The world of Elizabethan and Jacobean England was a world of growth and change. The great increase in the middle class, and in the population as a whole, demanded a new economy and means of livelihood, a new instrument of government (one recognizing "rights" and changed class structure), a new social code and a broad base of entertainment. The invention of printing a century before had contributed to that broader base, but it was the theater that supplied the more immediate needs of the greatest numbers. The theater grew and along with it came less-educated, more money-conscious writers, who gave the people what they wanted: entertainment. But Shakespeare, having passed through a brief period of hack writing, proceeded to set down important ideas in memorable language throughout most of his career. His plays, particularly the later ones, have been analyzed by recent critics in terms of literary quality through their metaphor, verse-line, relationships with psychology and myth, and elaborate structure. Yet Shakespeare was a man of the stage, and the plays were written to be performed. Only this will fully account for the humor of a deadly serious play like *Hamlet* or the spectacle of a *Coriolanus*.

Life in London

During Shakespeare's early years there, London was a walled city of about 200,000, with seven gates providing access to the city from the east, north, and west. It was geographically small and crisscrossed by narrow little streets and lanes. The various wards each had a parish church that dominated the life of the close-knit community. To the south and outside were slums and the haunts of criminal types, and farther out were the agricultural lands and huge estates. As the population increased and the central area declined, the fashionable people of the city moved toward the west, where the palace of Westminster lay. Houses were generally rented out floor by floor and sometimes room by room. Slums were common within the city, too, though close to pleasant enough streets and squares. "Merrie Olde England" was not really clean, nor were its people, for in those days there were no sewers or drains except the gutter in the middle of the street, into which garbage would be emptied to be floated off by the rain to Fleet ditch or Moor ditch. Plague was particularly ravaging in 1592, 1593-94 (when the theaters were closed to avoid contamination) and 1603. Medical knowledge, of course, was slight; ills were "cured" by amputation, leeching, blood-letting and cathartics. The city was (and still is) dominated by St. Paul's Cathedral, around which booksellers clustered on Paternoster Row.

Religious Atmosphere

Of great significance for the times was religion. Under Elizabeth, a state church had developed; it was Protestant in nature and was called Anglican (or today, Episcopalian) but it had arisen from Henry VIII's break with the Pope and from a compromise with the Roman Catholics who had gained power under Mary Tudor.

The Church of England was headed by the Archbishop of Canterbury, who was to be an increasingly important figure in the early part of the seventeenth century. There were also many schismatic groups, which generally desired further departures from Roman Catholicism. Calvinists were perhaps the most numerous and important of the Protestant groups. The Puritans, who were Calvinist, desired to "purify" the church of ritual and certain dogmas, but during the 1590's they were lampooned as extremists in dress and conduct.

Political Milieu

During Shakespeare's lifetime there were two monarchs: Elizabeth, 1558-1603, and James I, 1603-1625. Elizabeth was the daughter of Henry VIII and Anne Boleyn, his second wife, who was executed in 1536. After Henry's death, his son by his third wife, Jane Seymore (died in 1537), reigned as Edward VI. He was followed by Mary Tudor, daughter of Henry's first wife, Catherine of Aragon. Mary was a Roman Catholic, who tried to put down religious dissension by persecution of both Protestants and Catholics. Nor did her marriage to Philip II of Spain endear her to the people.

Elizabeth's reign was troubled by many offers of marriage, particularly from Spanish and French nobles — all Roman Catholic — and by the people's concern for an heir to the throne. English suitors generally canceled one another out by intrigue or aggressiveness. One of the most prominent was the Earl of Essex, Robert Devereux, who fell in and out of favor; he apparently attempted to take over the reins of control, only to be captured, imprisoned and executed in February, 1601. One claimant to the throne was Mary of Scotland, a Roman Catholic and widow of Francis II of France. She was the second cousin of Elizabeth, tracing her claim through her grandmother, who was Henry VIII's sister. Finally, settlement came with Elizabeth's acceptance of Mary's son as heir apparent, though Mary was to be captured, tried and executed for treason in 1587. Mary had abdicated the throne of Scotland in 1567 in favor of her son, James VI. His ascent to the throne of England in 1603 as James I joined the two kingdoms for the first time, although Scotland during the seventeenth century often acted independently of England.

Contemporary Events

Political and religious problems were intermingled in the celebrated Gunpowder Plot. Angry over fines that were levied upon those not attending Church of England services — primarily Roman Catholics — and offended by difficulties over papal envoys, a group of Catholics plotted to blow up Parliament, and James with it, at its first session on November 5, 1605. A cache of gunpowder was stored in the cellar, guarded by various conspirators, among them Guy Fawkes. The plot was discovered before it could be carried out and Fawkes, on duty at the time, was apprehended. The execution of the plotters and the triumph of the anti-Papists led in succeeding years to celebrations in the streets and the hanging of Fawkes in effigy.

Among the most noteworthy public events during these times were the wars with the Spanish, which included the defeat of the Spanish Armada in 1588, the battle in the Lowlands in 1590-1594, the expedition to Cadiz under Essex in 1596 and the expedition to the Azores (the Islands Expedition), also under Essex, in 1597. With trading companies especially set up for colonization and exploitation, travel excited the imagination of the people: here was a new way of life, here were new customs brought back by the sailors and merchants, here was a new dream world to explore.

In all, the years from around 1590 to 1601 were trying ones for English people, relieved only by the news from abroad, the new affluence and the hope for the future under James. Writers of the period frequently reflect, however, the disillusionment and sadness of those difficult times.

The Elizabethan Theater

Appearance

The Elizabethan playhouse developed from the medieval inn with its rooms grouped around a courtyard into which a stage was built. This pattern was used in The Theatre, built by James Burbage in 1576: a square frame building (later round or octagonal) with a square yard, three tiers of galleries, each jutting out over the one below, and a stage extending into the middle of the yard, where people stood or sat on improvised seats. There was no cover over the yard or stage and lighting was therefore natural. Thus performances were what we might consider late matinees or early evening performances; in summer, daylight continues in London until around ten o'clock.

Other theaters were constructed during the ensuing years: The Curtain in 1577, The Rose in 1587 (on Bankside), The Swan in 1595 (also Bankside) and Shakespeare's playhouse, The Globe, in 1599 (not far from The Rose). There is still some question about the exact dimensions of this house, but it seems to have been octagonal, each side measuring about 36 feet, with an over-all diameter of 84 feet. It was about 33 feet to the eaves, and the yard was 56 feet in diameter. Three sides were used for backstage and to serve the needs of the players. There was no curtain or proscenium, hence the spectators became part of the action. Obviously, the actors' asides and soliloquies were effective under these conditions.

There was no real scenery and there were only a few major props; thus the lines of the play had to reveal locations and movement, changes in time or place, etc. In this way, too, it was easier to establish a nonrealistic setting, for all settings were created in words. On either side of the stage were doors, within the flooring were trapdoors (for entrances of ghosts, etc.), and behind the main stage was the inner stage or recess. Here, indoor scenes (such as a court or a bedchamber) were played, and some props could be used because the inner stage was usually concealed by a curtain when not in use. It might also have served to hide someone behind the ever-present arras, like Polonius in *Hamlet*. The "chamber" was on the second level, with windows and a balcony. On the third level was another chamber, primarily for musicians.

Actors

An acting company such as the Lord Chamberlain's Men was a fellowship of ten to fifteen sharers with some ten to twelve extras, three or four boys (often to play women's roles) who might become full sharers, and stagehands. There were rival companies, each with its leading dramatist and leading tragic actor and clown. The Lord Admiral's Men, organized in 1594, boasted Ben Jonson and the tragedian Edward Alleyn. Some of the rivalry of this War of the Theaters is reflected in the speeches of Hamlet, who also comments on the ascendancy and unwarranted popularity of the children's companies (like the Children of Blackfriars) in the late 1590's.

The company dramatist, of course, had to think in terms of the members of his company as he wrote his play. He had to make use of the physical features and peculiar talents of the actors, making sure, besides, that there was a role for each member. The fact that women's parts were taken by boys imposed obvious limitations on the range of action. Accordingly, we often find women characters impersonating men; for example, Robert Goffe played Portia in *The Merchant of Venice*, and Portia impersonates a male lawyer in the important trial scene. Goffe also played Juliet, and Anne in *Richard III*, and Oberon in *Midsummer-Night's Dream*. The influence of an actor on the playwright can be seen, on the one hand, by noting the "humor" characters portrayed so competently by Thomas Pope, who was a choleric Mercutio in *Romeo*, a melancholic Jaques in *As You Like It*, and a sanguinary Falstaff in *Henry IV*, Part I; and by comparing, on the other hand, the clown Bottom in *Midsummer-Night's Dream*, played in a frolicsome manner by William Kempe, with the clown Feste in *Twelfth Night*, sung and danced by Robert Armin. Obviously, too, if a certain kind of character was not available within the company, then that kind of character could not be written into the play. The approach was decidedly different from ours today, where the play almost always comes first and the casting of roles second. The plays were performed in a repertory system, with a different play each afternoon. The average life of a play was about ten performances.

History of the Drama

English drama goes back to native forms developed from playlets presented at Church holidays. Mystery plays dealt with biblical stories such as the Nativity or the Passion, and miracle plays usually depicted the lives of saints. The merchant and craft guilds that came to own and produce the cycles of plays were the forerunners of the theatrical companies of Shakespeare's time. The kind of production these cycles received, either as moving pageants in the streets or as staged shows in a churchyard, influenced the late sixteenth-century production of a secular play: there was an intimacy with the audience and there was a great reliance on words rather than setting and props. Similar involvement with the stage action is experienced by audiences of the arena theatre of today.

The morality play, the next form to develop, was an allegory of the spiritual conflict between good and evil in the soul of man. The *dramatis personae* were abstract virtues and vices, with at least one man representing Mankind (or Everyman, as the most popular of these plays was titled). Some modern critics see *Othello* as a kind of morality play in which the soul of Othello is vied for by the aggressively evil Iago (as a kind of Satanic figure) and passively good Desdemona (as a personification of Christian faith in all men). The Tudor interlude — a short, witty, visual play — may have influenced the subplot of the Elizabethan play with its low-life and jesting and visual tricks. In mid-sixteenth century appeared the earliest known English comedies, Nicholas Udall's *Ralph Roister Doister* and *Gammer Gurton's Needle* (of uncertain authorship). Both show the influence of the Roman comic playwright Plautus. Shakespeare's *Comedy of Errors*, performed in the 1590's, was an adaptation of Plautus' *Menaechmi*, both plays featuring twins and an involved story of confused identities. The influence of the Roman tragedian Seneca can be traced from Thomas Norton and Thomas Sackville in *Gorboduc* to *Hamlet*. Senecan tragedy is a tragedy of revenge, characterized by many deaths, much blood-letting, ghosts, feigned madness and the motif of a death for a death.

Shakespeare's Artistry

Plots

Generally, a Shakespearean play has two plots: a main plot and a subplot. The subplot reflects the main plot and is often concerned with inferior characters. Two contrasting examples will suffice: Lear and his daughters furnish the characters for the main plot of filial love and ingratitude, whereas Gloucester and his sons enact the same theme in the subplot; Lear and Gloucester both learn that outward signs of love may be false. In *Midsummer-Night's Dream*, the town workmen (Quince, Bottom *et al.*) put on a tragic play in such a hilarious way that it turns the subject of the play — love so strong that the hero will kill himself if his loved one dies first — into farce, but this in the main plot is the "serious" plight of the four mixed-up lovers. In both examples Shakespeare has reinforced his points by subplots dealing with the same subject as the main plot.

11

Sources

The plots of the Elizabethan plays were usually adapted from other sources. "Originality" was not the sought quality; a kind of variation on a theme was. It was felt that one could better evaluate the playwright's worth by seeing what he did with a familiar tale. What he stressed, how he stressed it, how he restructured the familiar elements — these were the important matters. Shakespeare closely followed Sir Thomas North's very popular translation of Plutarch's *Life of Marcus Antonius*, for example, in writing *Antony and Cleopatra*; and he modified Robert Greene's *Pandosto* and combined it with the Pygmalion myth in *The Winter's Tale*, while drawing the character of Autolycus from certain pamphlets written by Greene. The only plays for which sources have not been clearly determined are *Love's Labour's Lost* (probably based on contemporary events) and *The Tempest* (possibly based on some shipwreck account from travelers to the New World).

Verse and Prose

There is a mixture of verse and prose in the plays, partially because plays fully in verse were out of fashion. Greater variety could thus be achieved and character or atmosphere could be more precisely delineated. Elevated passages, philosophically significant ideas, speeches by men of high rank are in verse, but comic and light parts, speeches including dialect or broken English, and scenes that move more rapidly or simply give mundane information are in prose. The poetry is almost always blank verse (iambic pentameter lines without rhyme). Rhyme is used, however (particularly the couplet), to mark the close of scenes or an important action. Rhyme also serves as a cue for the entrance of another actor or some off-stage business, to point to a change of mood or thought, as a forceful opening after a passage of prose, to convey excitement or passion or sentimentality and to distinguish characters.

Shakespeare's plays may be divided into three general categories, though some plays are not readily classified and further subdivisions may be suggested within a category.

The History Play

The history play, or chronicle, may tend to tragedy, like *Richard II*, or to comedy, like *Henry IV*, Part I. It is a chronicle of some royal personage, often altered for dramatic purposes, even to the point of falsification of the facts. Its popularity may have resulted from the rising of nationalism of the English, nurtured by their successes against the Spanish, their developing trade and colonization, and their rising prestige as a world power. The chronicle was considered a political guide, like the popular *Mirror for Magistrates*, a collection of writings showing what happens when an important leader falls through some error in his ways, his thinking or his personality. Thus the history play counseled the right path by negative, if not positive, means. Accordingly, it is difficult to call *Richard II* a tragedy, since Richard was wrong and his wrongness harmed his people. The political philosophy of Shakespeare's day seemed to favor the view that all usurpation was bad and should be corrected, but not by further usurpation. When that original usurpation had been established, through an heir's ascension to the throne, it was to be accepted. Then any rebellion against the "true" king would be a rebellion against God.

Tragedy

Tragedy in simple terms meant that the protagonist died. Certain concepts drawn from Aristotle's *Poetics* require a tragic hero of high standing, who must oppose some conflicting force, either external or internal. The tragic hero should be dominated by a *hamartia* (a so-called tragic flaw, but really an *excess* of some character trait, e.g., pride, or *hubris*), and it is this *hamartia* that leads to his downfall and, because of his status, to the downfall of others. The action presented in the tragedy must be recognizable to the audience as real and potential: through seeing it enacted, the audience has its passion (primarily suffering) raised, and the conclusion of the action thus brings release from that passion (*catharsis*). A more meaningful way of looking at tragedy in the Elizabethan theater, however, is to see it as that which occurs when essential good (like Hamlet) is wasted (through disaster or death) in the process of driving out evil (such as Claudius represents).

Comedy

Comedy in simple terms meant that the play ended happily for the protagonists. Sometimes the comedy depends on exaggerations of man's eccentricities — comedy of humors; sometimes the comedy is romantic and far-fetched. The romantic comedy was usually based on a mix-up in events or confused identity of characters, particularly by disguise. It moved toward tragedy in that an important person might die and the mix-up might never be unraveled; but in the nick of time something happens or someone appears (sometimes illogically or unexpectedly) and saves the day. It reflects the structure of myth by moving from happiness to despair to resurrection. *The Winter's Tale* is a perfect example of this, for the happiness of the first part is banished with Hermione's exile and Perdita's abandonment; tragedy is near when the lost baby, Perdita, cannot be found and Hermione is presumed dead, but Perdita re-appears, as does Hermione, a statue that suddenly comes to life. Lost identities are established and confusions disappear but the mythic-comic nature of the play is seen in the reuniting of the mother, Hermione, a kind of Ceres, with her daughter, Perdita, a kind of Prosperina. Spring returns, summer will bring the harvest, and the winter of the tale is left behind — for a little while.

What is it, then, that makes Shakespeare's art so great? Perhaps we see in it a whole spectrum of humanity, treated impersonally, but with

13

kindness and understanding. We seldom meet in Shakespeare a weeping philosopher: he may criticize, but he criticizes both sides. After he has done so, he gives the impression of saying, Well, that's the way life is; people will always be like that — don't get upset about it. This is probably the key to the Duke's behavior in *Measure for Measure* — a most unbitter comedy despite former labels. Only in *Hamlet* does Shakespeare not seem to fit this statement; it is the one play that Shakespeare, the person, enters.

As we grow older and our range of experience widens, so, too, does Shakespeare's range seem to expand. Perhaps this lies in the ambiguities of his own materials, which allow for numerous individual readings. We meet our own experiences — and they are ours alone, we think — expressed in phrases that we thought our own or of our own discovery. What makes Shakespeare's art so great, then, is his ability to say so much to so many people in such memorable language: he is himself "the show and gaze o' the time."

OTHELLO
Plot Summary

Othello opens in the great and powerful city-state of Venice. It is late at night. Roderigo, a young gentleman and former suitor of Senator Brabantio's daughter, Desdemona, is angry with Iago, a soldier in the Venetian army. Iago knew about Desdemona's elopement with the leader of the Venetian forces, a Moor named Othello, yet, complains Roderigo, Iago did not tell him. Roderigo reminds Iago that he has said he hates the Moor, although he serves him. Iago agrees; he is burning with jealousy and hatred, for even though he has been Othello's ensign, he was passed over when Othello chose a lieutenant. The post has gone to a young man from Florence, Michael Cassio, whom Iago holds in great contempt because all he knows of soldiering he has learned out of books. Iago, on the other hand, is a veteran of many hard-fought campaigns. Iago tells Roderigo to awaken Desdemona's father and inform him that she has run off with the Moor.

The two stand before Brabantio's house and call to him. When he appears at a window, Iago takes great pleasure in telling him the news. But, before the old man comes running down, Iago leaves very quickly, telling Roderigo that as the Moor's trusted ensign it is not right that he should be involved. He must still pretend love and loyalty to Othello, who is about to embark for Cyprus with the army to fight the Turks.

A distraught Brabantio, with his servants, appears downstairs and demands to know where he may find Othello and his daughter. Roderigo agrees to take him to Othello.

In the next scene we find Othello himself with Iago and several attendants on another street. Now Iago is filling Othello's ear with Brabantio's reaction to his daughter's marriage. Iago warns Othello that her father will do whatever he can to take his daughter from the Moor.

Cassio enters to tell Othello that the duke of Venice has sent for him to come immediately, for there is news from Cyprus. A moment later the enraged Brabantio bursts upon the scene, along with several armed followers. But Othello will not allow his men to draw their swords against his father-in-law. Instead, they will all appear before the Duke. Brabantio is sure that the Duke will take his side against Othello.

However, the war news is urgent, and the Duke, who admires Othello, needs him to lead the Venetian forces. He listens to Othello's story of love, and then, when Desdemona appears and makes it clear that she now belongs to Othello, the Duke attempts to reconcile Brabantio, his daughter, and her husband, but to no avail. Brabantio will have no more to do with Desdemona, and will not even allow her to remain in his house while Othello is off to war. Desdemona decides to follow her husband to Cyprus. Othello leaves his bride in the care of her loyal maid, Emilia, and her husband, his most trusted friend, Iago. When the Moor and his bride go off to spend their last few hours alone together, Iago tells Roderigo not to give up hope for Desdemona; he still may win her, for she will undoubtedly soon tire of the Moor. When Roderigo, somewhat encouraged, leaves, Iago reveals in a soliloquy how deep is his hatred and jealousy of Othello, and he mulls over some way to destroy him, using another man he hates, Cassio, as the instrument.

The scene of the story now changes to the island of Cyprus. There has been a great storm at sea which has wrecked the Turkish fleet and held up Othello's arrival. Cassio's ship arrives first, and a short while later Desdemona lands, along with Emilia and Iago. Desdemona is concerned for Othello, and to take her mind off her worries Cassio engages her in lighthearted conversation. Iago, seeing how well they get on together, visualizes the crystallization of his plans. When the victorious Othello arrives at last and goes off happily with his bride, Iago tells Roderigo he is convinced that it is really Cassio whom Desdemona loves. Skilfully, Iago induces Roderigo to pick a quarrel with Cassio that same evening.

Shortly afterwards a herald appears and announces that the night will be given over to feasting and celebration in honor of Othello's victory and, belatedly, for the married couple.

Later that night, Cassio is left in charge of the night watch while Othello and Desdemona retire to their chambers. Iago plies Cassio with wine and teases him in song until his mood becomes irritable. Then Roderigo appears according to plan and begins to fight with Cassio. Montano, the former governor of the island, tries to stop the fight and is wounded by the drunken Cassio.

Othello appears, and when he is told what happened he removes Cassio from his post. Cassio, now quite sober and sorry for all the trouble, is about to plead with Othello, but Iago quickly persuades him that his chances will be better if he asks Desdemona to intercede for him with her husband. He helps Cassio to arrange to meet Desdemona privately, and the softhearted girl promises Cassio she will do everything she can to restore him to Othello's good graces.

As Cassio is leaving, Iago and Othello appear. Othello notices Cassio's speedy departure, and Iago quickly seizes the opportunity to point out that Cassio seemed to be trying to avoid the Moor. Desdemona immediately and enthusiastically begins to beg Othello to pardon Cassio, and will not stop until Othello agrees.

The moment she and Emilia leave, however, Iago begins to plant seeds of doubt and suspicion in Othello's mind. Over and over again, all the while pretending to speak plainly and honestly, Iago subtly suggests that Desdemona and Cassio are having a love affair. When Iago is gone, and Desdemona returns, she finds her formerly gentle and loving husband in an overwrought emotional condition. She tries to soothe him by rubbing his head with her handkerchief, but he angrily throws it to the ground and leaves.

A while later, Emilia finds the handkerchief, and gives it to Iago. It is a very special handkerchief, embroidered with a strawberry pattern, and was Othello's first present to Desdemona. Then Othello returns, demanding of Iago some proof of his wife's infidelity. The quick-witted Iago, thinking of the handkerchief in his pocket, says that he overheard Cassio talk in his sleep about Desdemona, and that he had often noticed Cassio wiping his face with a strawberry-embroidered handkerchief. Othello is now convinced, and angrily vows revenge against both Cassio and his faithless wife. He promotes 'honest' Iago to lieutenant in Cassio's place.

Now Othello cannot wait to ask Desdemona where the handkerchief is, and when she cannot produce it he flies into a rage of jealousy. Meanwhile Iago has left the handkerchief where Cassio cannot fail to find it. He then arranges for Othello to actually see the handkerchief in Cassio's possession. Othello and Iago agree that Othello will kill Desdemona and Iago will dispose of Cassio. At this moment Lodovico arrives from Venice with orders for Othello to return at once, leaving Cassio as Governor of Cyprus. Events move swiftly to a climax as Othello accuses Desdemona and refuses to believe her protestations of innocence. He orders her to go to bed unattended.

Iago meanwhile persuades the gullible Roderigo to kill Cassio. Later that night, they attack Cassio on the street. However, things do not work out as Iago has planned, for it is Cassio who wounds Roderigo. Iago rushes out and stabs Cassio in the leg. Othello, hearing Cassio's cries for help, believes that half the revenge is completed and hastens to fulfill his end of things. But neither Cassio nor Roderigo is dead, and Iago, fearful that Roderigo will talk, kills him. Emilia enters and is sent off to tell Othello what has happened.

Othello, deaf to Desdemona's pleas and prayers, has smothered her in her bed. Emilia tries to get into the room, but not until he is sure that his wife is dead will Othello unlock the doors and let Emilia enter. He tells her what he has done. Stricken with horror, Emilia tells him that Iago's accusations were all lies, and she runs for help. The others enter and Othello, stunned, explains why he has killed Desdemona. Emilia tells him that it was she who took the fateful handkerchief and gave it to her husband. Iago stabs and kills her, and is himself wounded by the Moor, who, remorseful and heartbroken, stabs himself, and dies, falling on Desdemona's body.

Sources of the Play

Othello was performed at Whitehall Palace by Shakespeare's company on November 1, 1604, as we learn from an entry in the Revels Accounts. To have been chosen for representation at Court, the play must already have proved successful on the public stage. The question arises, then, as to how early it was composed. Since it draws upon material contained in Philemon Holland's English translation of Pliny's *Natural History*, issued in 1601, we can be sure it was written after the publication of that book. A few phrases from *Othello* are contained in the unauthorized, garbled First Quarto text of *Hamlet*, which was published in 1603; and their presence may indicate that *Othello* was in existence in that year. Most scholars agree that it was Shakespeare's next tragedy after *Hamlet*. Probably it was composed in 1602 or 1603.

Shakespeare apparently drew several details mentioned in *Othello* — the anthropophagi, the sulphur mines, the Pontic Sea, etc. — from the aforementioned Pliny's *Natural History*. And a few others he got from Sir Lewes Lewkenor's translation of *The Commonwealth and Government of Venice* by Cardinal Contareno. The plot, however, he found in Giraldi Cinthio's *Hecatommithi*. This he probably read in the original Italian or in Gabriel Chappuys' French translation of 1584.

A comparison of Shakespeare's play with Cinthio's novella reveals that the playwright has made a number of changes. For one thing, the main characters, merely sketched in the Italian work, are developed much more fully in the play. In the novella these characters, except for Desdemona, are nameless, being referred to simply as "the Moor," "the ensign," "the captain," etc. Shakespeare gives each a name: Othello, Iago, Cassio, etc. He invents the character Roderigo for the practical purpose of giving Iago someone to talk to concerning his evil plans and by so doing to reveal the malign side of his nature that he keeps hidden from the other characters. Thus an excessive use of self-revelatory soliloquies by Iago is avoided. Shakespeare fashions the one woman, Bianca, out of two in his source. He eliminates the ensign's little daughter from the story; as Granville-Barker comments, it would be difficult to image Iago as a fond father!

The elopement of Desdemona and Othello has no counterpart in the novella; there we are simply told that Desdemona married the Moor despite the opposition of her parents. In the play the elopement is an addition by Shakespeare devised to get the play under way and to help create a sense of the rapid passage of time. The hasty dispatch of Othello to Cyprus to defend the island against the Turks — another invention of the playwright—serves the same purpose and also tends to emphasize the esteem in which Othello is held as a soldier. In Cinthio's story, the Moor is merely sent to Cyprus when the garrison is changed there; Venice is not then at war.

The pace of the action in the play is different from that in the novella. It is clear from references in Cinthio's work that the action there is thought of as extending over a long period. Though Shakespeare's time references are ambiguous, the impression left upon the audience is that the time span in the play is shorter than that in the Italian story. The action certainly moves at a swifter pace. Scene follows scene with no chance for relaxation on the part of the spectators, and Shakespeare is thus able to achieve an emotional intensity lacking in his source.

One final difference between the two works may be noted. It concerns the motivation of Iago. In Cinthio, the villain hates Desdemona because she has not responded to his advances, and his plot is initially directed against her. In Shakespeare, it is Othello whom he hates and against whom he seeks revenge.

Othello As Tragedy

Fairly early in his career Shakespeare wrote *Romeo and Juliet*, which is a tragedy of fate. In this type of tragedy the hero experiences suffering and death because fate decrees that he shall, not because of any fault of his. As the playwright matured, however, he developed a concept of tragedy close to that set forth in Aristotle's *Poetics*, and he wrote dramas which we call tragedies of character. *Hamlet, Othello, King Lear, Macbeth, Coriolanus,* and *Antony and Cleopatra* are of this type.

In a tragedy of character, though the hero may be in outward conflict with an opposing force, the ultimate cause of his downfall lies within himself. Some character defect—or "tragic flaw," as it has come to be called—causes him to act in such a manner as to bring about his own misfortune, suffering, and death. This flaw may be brought into play by an external influence, such as the witches in *Macbeth*, but the flaw itself is innate. Aristotle speaks of this defect as an error of judgment; in Shakespeare's heroes it often takes the form of a passion which gets out of bounds, as, for example, Macbeth's ambition, Lear's egotism, Coriolanus' pride. Whatever the defect, by the end of the play there comes to the hero a clear realization that he has been at fault and that his suffering, at least in part, is of his own making.

Despite his flaw, the tragic hero, as described by Aristotle and as conceived by Shakespeare, possesses traits worthy of admiration. He is an exceptional person of great ability and reputation. In Shakespeare's plays he is a man of high position—a nobleman or a state leader. (Lear, for instance, is a king; Brutus, a Roman statesman.) Because his downfall comes about partly as a result of his own actions, we can recognize the justice of it; yet because of his good traits, we feel sympathy for him; and, conscious of his qualities of greatness, we are stirred to awe and terror by his downfall. Because it purges us of our emotions of fear and pity and because it leads us—despite the hero's fall—to realize that man has a greatness about him, Shakespearean tragedy leaves the spectator feeling not downcast, but uplifted.

Othello is clearly of the type of tragedy we have been discussing. Othello's tragic flaw is jealousy, a failing aroused in him by Iago—first by innuendo, later by supposed proof of Desdemona's infidelity. The Moor's nature is not one easily given to jealousy, and he has had no previous experience in dealing with it. He has learned to control his other emotions, as we see from his refusal to let Iago stir him to anger against Roderigo (Act I, Sc. 2, 6) and from his calm dealing with Brabantio a little later in the play (Act I, Sc. 2, 59 ff.). But against the unaccustomed passion of jealousy he has no defence. It robs him of reason and moves him to violence. He kills the one he loves, only to learn of her innocence and to realize how wrong he has been.

We sympathize with Othello because, despite his jealousy, he is worthy of admiration. Like Shakespeare's other tragic heroes, he is a man in high place. Of royal descent, he is a great general and, for a time, the governor of Cyprus. He is esteemed by the Venetian Senate and is called upon for help when the state is in danger. Until Iago's poison has done its work, he is a good friend to Cassio, whom he loves. Even Iago speaks of his "constant, loving, noble nature" and dares think "he'll prove to Desdemona/A most dear husband." It is true that for a time his finer nature is degraded by his passion and that he treats Desdemona in an outrageous manner (Act IV, Sc. 2); but, the poison of jealousy gone, his true nature reasserts itself at the end of the play. He sees no other way to atone for the death of Desdemona but to execute himself. Such a man as this moves us to admiration and to a sense of loss.

The World of *Othello*

Every particular literary work has a particular world, and when we begin the experience of being present in that world—whether for a few hours or a few weeks—we must have a basic understanding of what is unique about that world. In a certain sense, though, every literary work has several worlds, depending on our point of view. There is of course the physical world or what we sometimes call the location of the action. There is the world as it is shaped by a group of particular people, or characters, in interaction. This is the major and predominantly psychological world of the work. And, finally, closely connected, is the emotional world of the play: what sort of pervasive atmosphere does the author develop? What are the dominant attitudes and tones which emerge in this particular world? In other words, before plunging headlong into the close summary and analysis of a play, the student should reflect on the world of the play in general—in our case, on the world of *Othello*.

The Physical World

Othello takes place in space and time. The play covers the actions of three days spent in two locations. Act I covers one day and takes place in Venice. There is an interval of time following the first act in which a voyage is made between Venice and Cyprus. Act II covers one day in Cyprus, and Acts III, IV, and V seem to cover only one more day, also in Cyprus. The play is moved in location because the Duke of Venice decides that Othello should be sent to Cyprus to defend the island against an expected invasion by the Turks. Historically, Cyprus became subservient to the republic of Venice in 1471. Almost a hundred years went by before the island was invaded in 1570 by the Turks under Selim the Second. The following year Cyprus was in fact conquered, and for a long time thereafter remained a part of the Turkish empire. When the larger location is established clearly in mind, one should try to realize that almost all of the action takes place on streets and in chambers of the government castle at Cyprus. This is the physical world of *Othello* as it is positioned in place and time and set against the background of historical facts bearing on the relationship between the republic of Venice and the island of Cyprus.

The World Shaped by the Characters

To a great extent, the world of *Othello* is determined by the characters, and, in particular, by Iago. Iago's original envy and annoyance are produced by Othello's promotion of the Florentine Michael Cassio to the position of lieutenant, which Iago has desired for a long time. Iago's first wrath becomes the "exciting action" of the play — the action which sets everything else in motion. Iago's disappointment leads to his schemes to replace Cassio and to harm Othello — and on these two developments hangs the basic development of the world of the play.

Shakespeare artfully employs soliloquies to establish the particular world of *Othello*. When the audience listens to Iago pour forth his hate and ambition, the world becomes increasingly grim. It is clear at an early point that the world of *Othello* is going to be dark and melancholy, filled with developing "problems" between the characters. The problems lead to anxiety which in turn establishes the sadness of the play. Othello's growing jealousy over Desdemona — who is so innocent — becomes a sad, then terrifying, then pitiful emotion in the eyes of the spectators. Desdemona's innocence and purity, her faithfulness and unblemished love, move the audience through a series of pivotal emotions. We feel the world of the play changing as the play develops — and the dark mood of the play arises because the world is changing for the worse. No one feels light or carefree when goodness is being slaughtered — even butchered — by evil. And the proud, but easily misled, Othello seems helpless as he struggles against the evil forces set in motion by the villainous Iago. This is a play about infidelity, although there is no infidelity in the play. This is a play about the power of evil and we must always bear in mind Iago's reply when asked, in the end, by Othello, why he had driven him to false jealousy and murder: "Demand me nothing. What you know, you know./ From this time forth I never will speak word" (Act V, Sc. 2, lines 303-304). Shakespeare does not attempt to answer the "why" of evil because he realizes that to do so would be alien to a human world in which no explanation of evil is offered. In any case, the world of the play is defined and described by the inherent relationships between Othello and Iago, Othello and Desdemona, Iago and Emilia, Othello and Cassio, Iago and Roderigo, and many lesser ones. The basic ideas of the play, the products of the world as it were, arise out of the various confrontations and problems established in the structurally planned development of human relationships. Human characteristics are the explanations for most of the characters' behavioral patterns, and although Shakespeare is not one to stop and

21

psychoanalyze along the way, he makes it perfectly clear that the human flaws of the characters are as much responsible for evil as anything else.

Reflecting the Real World

While it is sometimes feared that the world of *Othello* is private fiction, it seems more honest and logical to look for the relationship between the world of the play and the world at large. This is partly done by understanding the physical world of the play, locating the action in Venice and Cyprus, and underlining the human essentials at the center of the characters. For Shakespeare had no intention of creating a purely imaginary world; as Mark Van Doren has written, Shakespeare's worlds are not "irresponsible constructions," for Shakespeare never lost sight of the real world. Van Doren adds:

> The world was still more precious — the great one he never forgot, and the little one in which he knew how to imprison its voice and body. What he dealt in was existence, and his dealings were responsible, high-hearted, and humane . . . Skakespeare loved the world as it is. That is why he understood it so well; and that in turn is why, being the artist he was, he could make it over again into something so rich and clear.

"The world as it is" is reflected in *Othello* with great accuracy, but only to the extent that we witness human emotions surrounding events which could in fact happen. The emotional world of the play is determined by Othello's central jealousy and Iago's hatred (and, really, his own jealousy of both Cassio and Othello). The play's main emotions, in other words, are not very attractive ones, particularly in contrast to the feeble and unwarranted optimism personified in the loving and faithful wife, Desdemona. But the emotions are nevertheless real and to this extent Shakespeare has succeeded in showing life as it is — or could be, under certain circumstances.

Summaries and Commentaries by act and Scene
ACT I · SCENE 1

Summary

The scene is a street in Venice. Roderigo is a rich young Venetian, susceptible, easily swayed by the stronger character, Iago, whose only purpose in cultivating him is to get money from him.

Roderigo is reproaching Iago because, although he has bribed him well to help him in his courtship of Desdemona, the beautiful daughter of the Senator Brabantio, the lady has just eloped with Othello, a Moorish general in the service of the Venetian army.

Iago's purpose at the moment is to keep Roderigo's confidence and thereby retain control of the young simpleton's money. This he proceeds to do by telling Roderigo that he has as much reason to hate the Moor as Roderigo has. He protests that he knew nothing about the elopement — "If ever I did dream of such a matter, Abhor me." He goes on to tell Roderigo the story of his own slight by the Moor. Although his petition to be made Othello's lieutenant was supported by "three great ones of the city," it was ignored by the Moor. Instead, Cassio was chosen, a Florentine, not a Venetian, who, Iago says (but from the beginning we must remember that Iago is not always to be believed) knows little of practical fighting, although his knowledge of the theory of war, and his skill in mathematics, is great. So this "counter-caster" has been chosen as Othello's lieutenant, while he, Iago, has been given the inferior position of Othello's "ancient" — his ensign, or personal attendant.

This story has the desired effect of gaining Roderigo's sympathy. "By heaven, I rather would have been his hangman . . . I would not follow him then."

Iago goes on cynically to point out that military appointments are made by favoritism — "by letter and affection" — rather than for service and merit. He himself only follows Othello, he says, in order to be revenged for the slight — "to serve my turn upon him." In saying this, Iago is honest up to a point with Roderigo because it serves his purpose of allying them both against the Moor. He sneers at those who serve their masters well, only to be dismissed when worn out in service. On the other hand he speaks highly of those who merely pretend to perform their duties conscientiously, all the while in reality looking after their own interests. "These fellows have some soul; And such a one do I profess myself. . . . I am not what I am" — truly a description of Iago.

Roderigo regretfully sighs over the Moor's success in winning Desdemona — "What a full fortune does the thick-lips owe, If he can carry't thus!"

Iago, satisfied with his quieting of Roderigo's complaints, now urges the young man to wake Desdemona's father to tell him of the elopement. He shows delight and excitement at the prospect of spreading the alarming news — "Make after him. Poison his delight, Proclaim him in the streets." As Roderigo, easily led on, readily takes up the suggestion — "Here is her father's house; I'll call aloud" — Iago, with almost insane enthusiasm, urges him on — "Do, with like timorous accent and dire yell As when, by night and negligence, the fire Is spied in populous cities."

Roused by their cries, Brabantio appears at his window. Half asleep, he is confused. When Roderigo makes himself known, Brabantio reminds him that he has already been forbidden in the house, and accuses him of making a drunken disturbance. Iago meanwhile is unknown to Brabantio, but adds his share to the argument. Roderigo finally succeeds in making the old man understand that his daughter has eloped with Othello. Fully aroused now, the Senator, apprehensive because of a dream of some such disaster, stirs up his household to make a search.

Iago, delighted with the success of his plans so far, explains that he, Iago, must still appear outwardly to be dutiful to his general, for Othello's value and importance in the present Turkish wars make him too precious to Venice to be too severely punished even for marrying the Senator's daughter. As long as Othello is in high esteem in Venice, Iago frankly acknowledges to Roderigo that he wishes to be in favor with Othello. So he deputes the poor dupe Roderigo to lead Brabantio's search party to an inn, the Sagittary, where Othello and Desdemona are to be found. Iago himself will go ahead to join Othello there and thus appear friendly to him still.

As Iago leaves, Brabantio with his search party enter, acknowledging to Roderigo that his alarm *is* well founded. Although formerly he has refused to entertain Roderigo as a suitor for Desdemona — why, we are not told — he now welcomes his help. He appeals to him to support his theory that Othello must have used charms and supernatural means to win Desdemona. He even wishes that he had allowed Roderigo's suit — "would you had had her!" He willingly accepts Roderigo's offer to show him where the couple can be found — "Pray you, lead on . . . On, good Roderigo; I'll deserve your pains."

Commentary

The opening scene of the play is extremely important in *Othello* because of the large amount of information it presents us in only 184 lines. Roderigo is a somewhat simple-minded, wealthy young Venetian gentleman and opens the play by accusing Iago of not doing what he was paid to do, namely, to help him in his courtship of Desdemona. This provides Iago with the opportunity of making a long answer which sets the play in motion.

Both Roderigo and Iago feel that they have a serious grievance with Othello, and both men have tried to pay money to win their cause. Roderigo has been paying Iago to help him win Desdemona, and apparently, Iago has been paying the "three great ones of the city" to help him become Othello's lieutenant.

The key to Iago's character lies in his own words — "I am not what I am." There has been a great deal of discussion about the reasons for Iago's fiendish plotting against Othello. In this scene he says that he hates the Moor because he preferred Cassio in his choice of lieutenant, but are we to believe him, or is this simply a way of gaining Roderigo's trust and sympathies and making sure that he will "have his purse" again? William Hazlitt, in referring to Iago, says "Some persons . . . have thought this whole character unnatural, because his villainy is without a sufficient motive. Shakespeare, who was as good a philosopher as he was a poet, thought otherwise. He knew that the love of power, which is another name for the love of mischief, is natural to man . . . Iago in fact belongs to a class of character, common to Shakespeare and at the same time peculiar to him; whose heads are as acute and active as their hearts are hard and callous. . .Iago is an extreme instance of the kind; that is to say, of diseased intellectual activity, with the most perfect indifference to moral good or evil, or rather with a decided preference of the latter, because it falls more readily in with his favourite propensity, gives greater zest to his thoughts and scope to his actions. He is quite or nearly indifferent to his own fate as to that of others; he runs all risks for a trifling and doubtful advantage, and is himself the dupe and victim of ruling passion — an insatiable craving after action of the most difficult and dangerous kind . . . His gaiety, such as it is, arises from the success of his treachery; his ease from the torture he has inflicted on others. He is an amateur of tragedy in real life; and instead of employing his invention on imaginary characters . . . he takes the bolder and more desperate course of getting up his plot at home, casts the principal parts among his nearest friends and connections, and rehearses it in downright earnest, with steady nerves and unabated resolution.''

Of course this development of Iago's character does not all appear in the first scene but, with it in mind, his behavior throughout the play may be more readily studied.

Roderigo is important not for himself, but because he sets events in motion by his attempted courtship of Desdemona — by engaging Iago's help he prompts the villain to begin his long series of intrigues. He is credulous — he implicitly believes all that Iago tells him of his hatred of Othello — and indeed Iago is so plausible, and appears to be so frank about his own ambitions, that it would be difficult for a simple person to doubt him. Roderigo's part in this scene is to give Iago the opportunity to reveal himself to the audience. Apart from Iago he appears to have no friends. Brabantio has forbidden him to court Desdemona, for which there must have been some reason. Roderigo shows little real appreciation for Desdemona in expecting that she can be won by his wealth. He is, in fact, just a dupe, a gull.

Brabantio deserves our sympathy. To be roused from sleep to be told that his daughter has eloped with a man of another race is distressing. His superstition is shown in his words that he has had a dream — "This accident is not unlike my dream" — and the fact that he is convinced that the Moor has used magic charms — "Is there not charms By which the property of youth and maidhood May be abused?" However, such beliefs were common in those times. His influential position is evident — "At every house I'll call; I may command at most."

Notes

The first scene accomplishes the following:

1.   Gives the setting — the time and place of the play. The first act takes place in Venice, the last four on the island of Cyprus. This island

was subject to the republic of Venice, and was attacked by the Turks in 1570, which gives us the period of the play.

2. Iago, the villainous protagonist, reveals his nature to Roderigo and so to us; his animosity towards Othello creates an atmosphere of suspense and interest to prepare us for Othello himself.

3. We are warned from the beginning that Iago is seldom what he appears to be; everything he does is to be for his own advantage; all his words and actions have a purpose — to further his own interests.

4. In a sense Roderigo sets the play in motion by his accusations against Iago — Iago must justify himself in order to keep control of Roderigo and his money, and the first plan that comes to his mind is a plot against Othello, the motive of the play.

5. It shows Brabantio's influential position in Venice and so goes to show the strength of Desdemona's love for Othello in marrying a person of whom her father does not approve.

ACT I · SCENE 2

Summary

This scene shows us Iago carrying out his plan of pretending great loyalty to Othello — "show out a flag and sign of love" — while Othello is a figure of importance in Venice. Completely treacherous to Roderigo, he is evidently giving Othello a version of his conversation with the dupe which is designed to give the impression that Iago has been shocked by Roderigo's animosity towards Othello. "He prated, And spoke such scurvy and provoking terms Against your honour That, with the little godliness I have, I did full hard forbear him." Notice how Iago always contrives here to belittle himself just enough to give an impression of bluff honesty — "with the little godliness I have."

He then proceeds to shake Othello's confidence ever so slightly. "Are you fast married?" He reminds Othello that Brabantio, Desdemona's father, is of great influence in the state, and will no doubt do all he can to part the couple and revenge himself upon Othello.

Othello is confident; he knows that his services to Venice have been so valuable that they will "out-tongue" Brabantio's complaints. Also, although he hesitates to use this fact unless he must, he himself is of royal birth. Only his great love for Desdemona has persuaded him to give up his "unhoused free condition."

They are interrupted by the approach of a torchlight party. Iago, in his false character as Othello's friend, advises him to retire, for it may be Brabantio's search party. Othello, however, has no feeling of guilt, and is ready to meet them.

However, the coming party is a group of the Duke's officers, led by Cassio, the Florentine whom Othello has made his lieutenant — the appointment which Iago gives Roderigo as his reason for hating the Moor. Othello greets them graciously and hears from Cassio that the Duke has sent for him in great haste. There has been news from the

26

island of Cyprus, where the Turks are expected to attack. Already several consuls are assembled with the Duke, and such is Othello's importance that no less than three search parties have been sent out to summon him.

While Othello goes in, presumably to tell Desdemona the news, Cassio, seemingly ignorant of Othello's marriage, is about to learn of it from Iago when they are interrupted by Othello's reappearance. It is notable that there seems to be no outward show of ill-feeling by Iago towards Cassio in spite of his sentiments expressed to Roderigo.

As all set out for the Duke's council-chamber, Brabantio's party approaches. Again Iago warns Othello. Members of both parties draw their swords. Iago cunningly contrives to engage Roderigo in such a way that to Othello it appears that he is attacking the young man, while in reality he is drawing him aside to make sure that he will come to no harm — "You, Roderigo! come, sir, I am for you."

Othello is calm and undisturbed. "Keep up your bright swords, for the dew will rust them." With dignity he tells Brabantio that respect for his age has more effect than weapons.

Brabantio breaks out into an impassioned accusation against the Moor. His daughter must surely have been enchanted by Othello. It is impossible to believe that she, who had refused marriage with eligible young Venetians, would fly in the face of convention and marry a man of the Moor's terrifying appearance. He must have used magical arts to win her, and for so doing, Brabantio threatens to have him punished.

Othello, still calm, orders everyone to refrain from fighting. It is for him to decide when to take up arms. When Brabantio insists that Othello should go to prison to await judgment, Othello points out that the Duke has already summoned him. Brabantio seizes this opportunity of pleading his cause before the Duke, and all depart.

Commentary

Of the three scenes in the first act, the second is by far the shortest (99 lines). In terms of structure we must try to understand why Othello, as the title character, is introduced in this short second scene. It is necessary that the first scene deal with the background events and with a *view* of Othello, but we still wonder why Othello himself is not made to enter in the first scene. In any case, the second scene takes place on a different street in Venice, where Iago and Othello are walking together. They meet Cassio and certain officers carrying torches. Cassio explains that the Duke of Venice wishes to see Othello although he does not know why. Cassio suggests that there may be some new and serious news from Cyprus, for Othello is being sought with great energy by many search parties.

The scene manages to advance the plot with great facility. The idea of having the Senate called together over pressing matters in Cyprus at the same time that Brabantio and his men are out searching for Othello leads to a nice dilemma in the street. Furthermore, Iago's opening lines to Othello — that he would have struck Brabantio for making cruel remarks about Othello, except for his moral concern — establish his essential hypocrisy and evil even more openly. Othello's few lines are not that revealing — which is why they *are* significant, for, as a man of action and a good soldier, Othello should not be making lengthy speeches in the street to his aide Iago. Iago's quick sham of fighting with Roderigo reveals to us how cunning Iago can be on the spur of the moment; also, he utilizes one brief second alone with Cassio to begin to tell him about Othello's secret marriage. Iago, in other words, makes the most of every opportunity, and this enlarges our image of him as a Machiavellian schemer.

The mere fact that Othello is so willing to answer to any charges regarding his elopment with Desdemona makes us realize of course that he did not need to use any drugs or "magic." Early in the scene Othello points out to Iago that he is, after all, from royal ancestors ("I fetch my life and being/ From men of royal siege" [line 21]) and thus feels no guilt over his new marriage to someone as high-bred as Desdemona. And his final consent to go before Brabantio strengthens this relatively noble dimension of his character. Our whole introduction to him, in short, is a picture of simplicity combined with honor and honesty.

Notes

1.   Note the contrast of Othello's nature with that of Iago.

2.   This scene shows Iago in a different light from that in which he has shown himself to Roderigo. Here he is the apparently loyal ancient to Othello, adapting his performance to suit the person to whom he is speaking — revealing his evil versatility.

3.   Here, we get a picture of Othello's dignity and self-confidence in an emergency, as well as more background information about him.

4.   We learn of Othello's good reputation with the Duke and senators who send for him when an emergency arises.

5.   Through Brabantio's speech to Othello, we appreciate the unusual and courageous step which Desdemona has taken in marrying someone so far removed from her own natural environment.

ACT I · SCENE 3

Summary

While the events of the former scene have been taking place, the Duke of Venice is in council with his officers and senators. Three different reports have come, all giving the news that a fleet of Turkish vessels — enemies of Venice — is bearing towards the island of Cyprus. Although the reports differ in their details as to the number of vessels, it is evident that the main fact is true. Just as the authorities agree that it must be true that the Turks are approaching Cyprus, a sailor comes hastily with a conflicting report — the Turks are now heading for the island of Rhodes. This seems unlikely; Cyprus is the more important island and therefore the more likely object of the Turks' attack. More news arrives — the Turks have approached Rhodes only in order to join with another reinforcing fleet; now the whole force is on the way to Cyprus. During this mounting excitement, Brabantio and Roderigo, Othello, his lieutenant, and his ensign,Iago,enter.

The Duke greets Othello first, immediately enlisting his services against the Turkish threat. Only then does he notice Brabantio, whom he has already missed from the council. Brabantio, full of his own grief, passes lightly over the national emergency and pours out his personal sorrows to the Duke, once more accusing Desdemona's lover of winning her by unnatural, unlawful spells and medicines. The Duke is indignant and sympathetic, promising stern punishment for the offender. But when Othello's name is given, both Duke and senators express — not rage or horror — but regret that it is Othello who is thus accused. "We are very sorry for't" shows their regard for the Moor. The Duke does not turn upon him, but reasonably asks what he has to say.

Othello now describes his courtship of Desdemona. He acknowledges immediately that he has married Brabantio's daughter. He confesses that his life has been one of action rather than of culture, and that his only skill in speaking lies in his ability to describe "feats of broil and battle." However, he will attempt to tell by what "charms" he won his wife.

Brabantio interrupts to speak of his daughter, modest and quiet. To him it is inconceivable that she could fall in love with a man of Othello's startling appearance. Again he insists that the Moor must have "wrought upon her" with charms and drugs.

The Duke judicially points out that it is not enough to make such a charge; there must be proof. The first senator urges Othello to state his own case.

Before doing so, Othello asks to have Desdemona present so that her story may be heard too. While Iago goes to fetch her, Othello begins: Brabantio "loved me; oft invited me." Brabantio encouraged him to tell his adventures — accidents, escapes, slavery, life in strange places among outlandish peoples. Desdemona too would listen, in the moments she could take from her household duties. Noticing her interest, Othello contrived to have her beg him to tell her the whole story without interruption. His account of his experiences brought tears and sighs from her; she was distressed, yet full of admiration for the hero of these adventures, and she confessed that she could love such a man. Encouraged, then Othello told of his love — and this was the only "witchcraft" that brought about his success.

As Desdemona enters, the Duke remarks that such a tale would win his own daughter. He advises Brabantio to make the best of the matter. Brabantio, however, is not satisfied until he hears Desdemona speak —

if she confesses that she did indeed meet Othello half-way in the courtship, he will no longer blame the Moor.

Desdemona speaks out courageously — to her father she owes her life and her education, but to her husband Othello, she owes the same duty that her mother owed to her father, Brabantio.

Brabantio then brusquely puts her affairs aside, bitterly remarking that he would rather adopt a child than have one of his own. He urges the Duke to proceed with state affairs, and hands Desdemona into the care of Othello.

The Duke adds further advice — to the effect that "It is no use crying over spilt milk." Useless grieving harms only the griever. Brabantio sarcastically retorts that the same could apply in public as well as in private troubles — for instance, to the present attack on Cyprus by the Turks. Remarking that words are poor comfort, he begs the Duke to go on with public business.

The Duke clearly and concisely outlines the situation. The Turks are proceeding in full force against Cyprus. Although Montano is now in charge of the island, Othello is the one who knows its military conditions best, and for that reason he must put aside his private affairs for a time and take charge in this emergency.

Othello, the tried soldier, makes no objection, only asking that Desdemona shall be properly cared for during his absence. The Duke suggests that she should go back to her father's home; Brabantio, Othello and Desdemona herself feel that this would create an awkward and unpleasant situation. She begs the Duke to let her go to Cyprus with Othello, saying that her love for her husband depends upon his character and profession as a soldier. If she stays home all the things upon which her love rests will be taken from her.

Othello adds his pleas, promising that he will never neglect his duties for the sake of their love, which has a spiritual and intellectual basis.

The Duke and the senators, impatient to have matters arranged, agree, ordering Othello to leave for Cyprus that night, leaving behind a trustworthy officer to bring further orders and to be in charge of those following Othello later.

Othello suggests his ancient, Iago — "A man he is of honesty and trust" and further shows his confidence in Iago by leaving Desdemona in the care of Iago's wife, Emilia, until they meet in Cyprus.

The Duke and the senators leave, with good wishes and complimentary words to Othello — except Brabantio, who strikes an ominous note — "Look to her, Moor, if thou hast eyes to see; She has deceived her father, and may thee." These words are brought back to Othello's mind with telling force by Iago later in the play. However, now he has no doubts — "My life upon her faith!" Appealing to Iago (honest Iago!) to see that Desdemona is well attended by Emilia, he leads her away, leaving Iago alone with Roderigo, as they were in the first scene.

Much has happened since then; Roderigo is despondent at losing Desdemona. "I will incontinently drown myself." Iago is disgusted. He pours scorn upon Roderigo. He has no conception of real love himself, and has no patience for anyone who takes it seriously. He does not want to lose Roderigo's confidence (which would mean losing Roderigo as a source of money) and proceeds to win him over again with clever arguments. A man's will, he says, is superior to all his other faculties. Any feeling can be overcome by a man's will. Roderigo is still despondent; Iago continues to work upon him. "Be a man." He suggests that Desdemona will soon tire of Othello. Let Roderigo "put money in thy purse" and keep up his hope. He adds other insinuations — the Moor may change in his feelings; Desdemona may soon wish for a younger lover; a match between a barbarian and a highly civilized, sophisticated, subtle Venetian lady cannot last — it is ridiculous to talk of drowning oneself while there is still so much hope. Roderigo is persuaded at last by Iago's unfounded and wicked hints, and wishes to make sure that Iago will still help him. Iago, again impressing on him the need to raise more money, assures him that he hates the Moor as much as does Roderigo, and will enjoy carrying out revenge upon him. Taking it for granted that the young man is now in his grip once more, he dismisses him for a time. Roderigo is indeed duped once more — "I am changed. I'll go sell all my land."

Iago is pleased, but not surprised, by his success. The only reason he associates with "such a snipe" is for his own gain — "Thus do I ever make my fool my purse." Alone, he begins to make plans for involving Cassio in his intrigues — in order to increase his own self-importance and sense of power, ostensibly to "get even" with Cassio for being appointed lieutenant. He decides to hint to Othello that Cassio is too friendly with Desdemona. Possibly Brabantio's parting warning to Othello has given him the idea. Cassio is the right type of man to accuse of such misbehavior — handsome, well-mannered, friendly — one that people might easily suspect of being a ladies' man. Othello, reflects Iago, is not jealous by nature — "The Moor is of a free and open nature That thinks men honest that but seem to be so, And will as tenderly be led by the nose As asses are."

Delighted and excited by his evil plans, he closes the scene — "Hell and night Must bring this monstrous birth to the world's light."

Commentary

The third and final scene of Act I is much longer than Scenes 1 and 2 combined. It is the first scene of the play in which we begin to find long, dramatic speeches by the major characters, and these speeches are primarily generated by the whole idea of Brabantio's continuing accusations of Othello.

Brabantio is naturally in a state of great distress. His belief that Othello has used magical means to enchant his daughter seems ridiculous to modern minds, but is quite in keeping with the superstitions of his day. He is reasonable, when Desdemona confesses that she was "half the wooer" and makes no further protest against her joining Othello. His grief and regret at his daughter's conduct is what one would expect under the circumstances. He shows a bitter sense of humor in his retort to the Duke's would-be consolatory advice that the best way to lessen an injury is to take the trouble with a smile — "So let the Turk of Cyprus us beguile; We lose it not, so long as we can smile." Desdemona's deceit has shaken his confidence in her, and he warns Othello, "Look to her Moor, if thou hast eyes to see; she has deceived her father, and may thee."

The Duke is reasonable and judicious. He meets the alarming news about the Turkish attack with calmness and resource. His attitude towards Othello's courtship and marriage is understanding and sympathetic. His advice to Brabantio to make the best of the matter is wise, even though it is of no particular comfort to the bereaved father.

Othello's high reputation is continually dwelt upon in this scene. The rulers of the state welcome him, listen patiently to his explanation of his private affairs even while national safety is in the balance. They are willing to accept his version of the courtship. Even Brabantio, though hurt and grieved, abuses him no longer when the matter is explained, and speaks sorrowfully rather than in anger.

Although he calls himself "rude in speech," nevertheless his description of his wooing, and of the tales with which he "bewitched" Desdemona, show command of language, imagination, powers of description, and a clear way of presenting his facts with telling force.

A man of duty and action, he is ready to undertake the command of the Cyprus expedition immediately, only making sure that Desdemona will be taken care of. When Desdemona asks to accompany him, he is delighted, but stresses the fact that even her presence will not interfere with his duties.

His faith in Iago — and indeed in everyone — is complete. "A man he is of honesty and trust." "Honest Iago, My Desdemona must I leave to thee."

During the earlier part of the scene Iago is silent, no doubt treasuring up every word and circumstance that will be of the use to him in his plots. Brabantio's warning to Othello gives him an excellent instrument of torture to use upon Othello later.

Notice the quickness and ease with which Iago identifies himself and his cause with "all the tribe of hell," for some critics hold that Iago is no more nor less than the devil himself. Iago explains to Roderigo that he hates the Moor and hopes that perhaps Roderigo will be able to make Othello a cuckold; Roderigo would enjoy himself and Iago would be happy to see Othello hurt in this way.

Iago's full evil comes to the foreground as he stands center-stage all alone at the end of the scene and the act. He delivers a final soliloquy in which he announces his frank intention to secure Cassio's position, on the one hand, and to harm Othello on the other; he thinks perhaps he will suggest to Othello that there is a secret love affair between Desdemona and Cassio:

> I hate the Moor:
> And it is thought abroad, that 'twixt my sheets
> He hath done my office: I know not if't be true;
> But I, for mere suspicion in that kind,
> Will do as if for surety. He holds me well;
> The better shall my purpose work on him.
> Cassio's a proper man; let me see now,
> To get his place and to plume up my will
> In double knavery — How, how? — Let's see:—
> After some time, to abuse Othello's ear
> That he is too familiar with his wife.
> He hath a person and a smooth dispose
> To be suspected, framed to make women false   (lines 392-404).

Notes

1. During Othello's autobiographical account, mention is made of '*Anthropophagi*'. This is another name for cannibals, which Shakespeare probably picked up from Holland's translation of Pliny's *Natural History*. It was mostly as a result of describing his great adventures that Othello was able to win Desdemona's affections.

2. Note that Desdemona's attraction to Othello is two-fold: she worships his honour and his deeds, but at the same time she has an obvious sexual attraction to him. Throughout, Othello stresses that the relationship is based on intellectual and spiritual compatibility.

ACT II · SCENE I

Summary

The exposition or introduction is completed, and the second stage of the play begins with this scene — the complication or conflict, in which the tangled threads of the action are tied into a still tighter knot, and the action of the play rises to a higher peak of excitement and suspense.

The background is now the island of Cyprus, where Othello is to take command upon his arrival. Montano, the governor of the island, who is to be replaced by Othello, is awaiting his arrival with anxiety, for a terrific storm is raging. His two gentlemen attendants describe its fury — "The chidden billow seems to pelt the clouds . . . I never did like molestation view On the enchafed flood."

But "It is an ill wind that blows nobody good" — news comes that "The desperate tempest hath so bang'd the Turks That their designment halts" — the greater part of their fleet is wrecked.

This good news has been brought by Cassio, Othello's lieutenant, who has arrived safely. The storm has separated and delayed Othello's vessel, and the other on which Desdemona, Iago and his wife Emilia, and Roderigo are journeying.

Montano, although he is about to yield place to Othello, speaks generously and well of him, praying for his safe arrival. He suggests that they shall all go to the seaside to watch for the expected ships. However, Cassio enters, just as a shout arises of "a sail, a sail!" The townspeople, gathered at the sea-shore, have caught sight of a vessel, and there is a discharge of guns as a salute to its approach. During this excitement Cassio tells Montano of Othello's marriage, speaking in glowing terms of Desdemona's charms.

It is Iago's vessel that has just put in; Cassio, again in extravagantly metaphorical language, attributes his safety to the fact that "the divine Desdemona" has been on board.

However, in spite of his rather artificial expressions, he is sincere, and utters a fervent prayer for Othello's safety. "Great Jove, Othello guard."

Desdemona, Emilia, Iago, Roderigo and their attendants enter at this moment, and Cassio continues his enthusiastic admiration — "Ye men of Cyprus, let her have your knees."

Desdemona acknowledges their greeting, but her first thought is of Othello "What tidings can you tell me of my lord". . .O, but I fear—"

But there is another cry and a salvo of guns, signifying the approach of another ship. While someone goes to investigate, Cassio warmly greets Emilia, explaining to Iago as he kisses her that such a greeting is simply an example of his good breeding. Iago is indifferent and scornful — remarking that Emilia has a sharp tongue, and uses it too constantly. When Desdemona defends Emilia, Iago discourteously includes her in his criticism of women. Again he is playing the bluff, outspoken soldier's part.

Desdemona can actually think of nothing but her anxiety about Othello, but to distract her own mind from this she enters into a bantering play of words with Iago. Her mind is not completely upon the game — she breaks off to ask "There's one gone to the harbour?" Iago climaxes the playful interchange of questions and answers by a long description of a deserving woman — lines 148-168 — and follows it by the anti-climax — such a wonderful woman is fit only to raise children and keep her household accounts.

Desdemona shows her amused impatience with his cynical attitude by warning Emilia not to pay any attention to his lessons; then she turns to Cassio to ask his opinion. As they speak together, Iago malignantly observes them. Cassio gallantly takes Desdemona's hand as they talk; Iago deliberately misinterprets his courtesy and gloats over the possibility of making his behavior show in the worst possible light, as evidence that he, Cassio, is making love to his general's wife.

There is a sound of trumpets and Othello and his attendants enter. He and Desdemona are reunited joyfully. At this point in the play,

Othello's happiness is at its height — he has come safely through fearful dangers to meet Desdemona again; as yet Iago has not been able to begin to undermine his confidence in her. "If it were now to die, 'Twere now to be most happy; for, I fear, My soul hath her content so absolute That not another comfort like to this Succeeds in unknown fate." Desdemona is full of hope for an even happier future. Iago is filled with fiendish delight at the prospect of destroying their happiness. "O, you are well tuned now! But I'll set down the pegs that make this music, As honest as I am."

Once more Iago is left with Roderigo. His plotting is directly against Cassio—but with indirect and horrible results and effects upon Othello and Desdemona. One plan involves the other. Iago tells Roderigo that Desdemona is in love with Cassio; that already she has begun to tire of Othello and is turning towards the younger, more attractive lieutenant. He praises Cassio's appearance and manners — surely Desdemona must find him irresistible! Roderigo protests faintly, but Iago easily persuades him that Desdemona's and Cassio's innocent conversation had a sinister significance. "They met so near with their lips that their breaths embraced together. Villainous thoughts, Roderigo!"

So now Roderigo, always ready to believe Iago, is jealous not only of Othello but of Cassio. Therefore it is easy for Iago to persuade Roderigo to help in getting rid of this new rival. Iago's scheme involves Roderigo as his tool, while he himself will run no risk. Roderigo is to take command that night, by Iago's orders. He is to annoy Cassio in some way, "by speaking too loud, or tainting his discipline." Cassio, says Iago, is hot-tempered and will likely attack Roderigo. There will be a quarrel, and on the strength of it, Iago will contrive to have the Cyprians mutiny against Cassio and demand his dismissal.

Roderigo swallows the bait and promises to carry out Iago's suggestions. Iago as usual thinks aloud and makes further plans in a soliloquy which closes the scene. By now he has persuaded himself that Cassio loves Desdemona; even that she loves him. Iago's great difficulty is his knowledge of Othello's nobility — "The Moor, howbeit that I endure him not, Is of a constant, loving, noble nature, And I dare think he'll prove to Desdemona A most dear husband." But a new thought occurs to Iago — in fact a whole new situation. Now he says that he himself loves Desdemona; that also he suspects Othello of making love to his wife Emilia. He will not be satisfied until he can "put the Moor At least into a jealousy so strong That judgment cannot cure." He gives so many reasons for his actions that it is hard to believe any one is the true one. He even suspects that Cassio too has made love to Emilia. As he says — "'Tis here, but yet confused; Knavery's plain face is never seen till used." He is determined to practise upon Othello's "peace and quiet even to madness" — but how, or exactly why, is certainly confused as yet.

Commentary

Montano is not an important character in the development of the play — his interest here lies in the fact that he regards Othello so highly and thereby adds to our impression of the Moor.

Othello is shown here at the very height of his good fortune. It is a period of calm happiness between the storms through which he has just safely passed, and the tragic times to come. Unconsciously he expresses this circumstance in his words to Desdemona "I fear . . . That not another comfort like to this Succeeds in unknown fate."

Cassio speaks in high-flown, picturesque language, using many figures of speech. Although his manner of speaking is exaggerated, he is sincere in his hero-worship of his general Othello and his enthusiastic but respectful admiration of Desdemona. His demonstrative greeting and gallantry are not, as Iago would suggest, based upon any unlawful feelings toward Desdemona — they arise from his youth and impetuosity and desire to show courtesy.

As a loving wife, Desdemona thinks entirely of Othello. Her interlude with Iago, as well as introducing a little comic relief into the tense atmosphere of the scene, goes to show her control over her feelings in a time of anxiety — "I am not merry; but I do beguile The thing I am by seeming otherwise."

Iago treats his own wife contemptuously; he has a low opinion of women in general and does not hesitate to express it, although to Desdemona he does so in a more subtle manner. He has a purpose even in this — his out-spokenness, he knows, will strengthen the impression he wishes others to have of him, of "honest Iago." His true nature is revealed in the comments he makes, unheard by the others, upon the conversation between Cassio and Desdemona — a combination of his own evil interpretation of an innocent encounter and his wishes that that interpretation is a true one. There is a continual struggle going on within him — much against his will, he realizes that certain other people are really good, without any purpose in being so; he despises them for it, and yet cannot help occasionally contrasting them with himself. As he says later in the play, of Cassio "He hath a daily beauty in his life That makes me ugly."

His persuasion of Roderigo is clever — more clever than it needs to be for a such a gullible person, but Iago seems to enjoy playing upon his gullibility; it is good practice for more difficult tasks. Again he discloses his contempt of women, even of Desdemona — for although he tells himself he loves her, it is not the pure love which Othello feels for her. His scheme to have Roderigo do his contemptible work for him in getting rid of Cassio is sharp and unscrupulous, and shows his disregard for Roderigo. He allows his imagination full play in his soliloquy, accusing Cassio, Desdemona, and Othello in turn of infidelity. His almost insane desire to do evil is well expressed in his own words—" 'Tis here, but yet confused; Knavery's plain face is never seen till used."

Notes

This scene has several purposes:

1. To introduce the first complication, whereby Cassio is to be accused of making love to Desdemona, and also to be drawn into a quarrel by Roderigo so that he may be dismissed from his post as Othello's lieutenant.

2. The excitement of the storm and the arrival of the three vessels suggests an outward counterpart to the stormy emotions of the characters involved in the drama.

3. The happiness of Othello and Desdemona at meeting safely again brings their emotions to a height from which the plotting of Iago will gradually but surely drag them down — there will be dramatic contrast.

4. The conversation between Desdemona and Iago serves a dramatic purpose by drawing out the suspense felt concerning Othello. There is also strong dramatic contrast — Iago feels no apprehension and enjoys the clever questions and retorts. Desdemona, however, takes part only to distract her mind from her anxiety about her husband — only the surface of her mind is engaged in the conversation.

5. Cassio's conversation with Desdemona is the turning point in this scene — it gives Iago plenty of material with which to work his schemes. His description is enough to make Roderigo believe that the two are in love.

6. Iago's plans are advancing rapidly — his soliloquy at the end shows how one evil scheme can lead to another in the mind of a man so cold-blooded and cunning.

ACT II · SCENE 2

Summary

This is simply a proclamation, read by a herald to a crowd of people. Othello has ordered a night of general rejoicing and merry-making, to celebrate the destruction of the Turkish fleet, and to do honor to his marriage. Bonfires, dances and feasts are to be held from five o'clock until eleven.

Commentary

This very brief scene establishes the action of the play in Cyprus. The war is over, Othello is now governor of the island and is happily married. The coming celebrations, as the following scene will show, present Iago with the perfect opportunity to carry out his plans against Cassio.

ACT II · SCENE 3

Summary

It is about five hours since the herald read the proclamation. There has been plenty of time for merrymaking, feasting and drinking. Othello is speaking affectionately to Cassio as they enter a hall in the castle with Desdemona, pointing out that they must not let their celebrations interfere with their duty. Cassio promises to keep an eye on the guard, even though Iago is on duty too. Iago enters as Othello and Desdemona leave.

Cassio remarks that they must look to the watch. Iago, however, protests that it is still early, "not yet ten o'clock"—and the proclamation has given them until eleven to relax. He reminds Cassio that the celebrations are in honor of Desdemona, and so cleverly brings her into their conversation. By making complimentary remarks about her, he encourages Cassio to do the same, although Cassio's references to her are respectful as well as admiring. "An inviting eye; and yet methinks right modest."

Iago then proposes that they will drink a stoup of wine with two Cyprus gallants who wish to toast Othello's health. Cassio realizes that he has had enough already—only one cup, but quite sufficient for him, for he is easily affected by it. Iago urges that it is a night for revelry and persuades Cassio to bring in the two gallants. While Cassio yields unwillingly, Iago indulges in one of his soliloquies, planning further mischief, and reviewing what he has done already. If Cassio has another drink, he will be in a quarrelsome mood, just as Iago wishes. Roderigo already has drunk so many toasts to Desdemona that he is in no state to keep the watch, as he must do. Along with him there will be three young men of Cyprus, also befuddled with drink. This is an ideal situation for Iago's purpose—to set Cassio amongst them so that trouble is bound to arise for him.

Cassio re-enters with Montano, the former governor of Cyprus, and with other gentlemen. Servants are bringing in wine for them. Evidently while Iago has been soliloquizing, Cassio has already had more to drink—"'Fore God, they have given me a rouse already." Iago here plays the part of a jolly, convivial fellow, encouraging Cassio to drink more, singing and leading Cassio on. Cassio is beginning to show the effects already; he protests too elaborately that he is not drunk, with exaggerated carefulness that shows he is not himself—"Do not think, gentlemen, I am drunk. This is my ancient; this is my right hand, and this is my left. I am not drunk now; I can stand well enough, and speak well enough."

As he goes out, Iago turns to Montano and proceeds to impress Cassio's condition upon Montano—pretending great regard for Cassio, and regret that he has such a weakness. "He is a soldier fit to stand by Caesar And give direction; and do but see his vice . . . I fear the trust Othello puts him in, On some odd time of his infirmity, Will shake this island."

Montano is concerned — "But is he often thus?" Iago, lying, assures him that Cassio cannot sleep at night unless he drinks at bed time. Montano is shocked, and thinks that Othello should know of this. Iago hypocritically protests that he would never inform against Cassio — "Not I, for this fair island" but he is quite sure that thanks to his insinuations, the news will be spread. Montano will unwittingly help him.

They are interrupted by a cry of "Help!" Iago's scheme has succeeded. Cassio rushes in, pursuing Roderigo and abusing him violently. He strikes him. Montano interferes, trying to stop the quarrel; he tells Cassio that he is drunk. Cassio, furious, attacks Montano. This is even better than Iago had hoped; he begs Cassio to stop fighting, knowing perfectly well that in Cassio's condition his words will not be heeded.

Aroused by the noise and confusion, Othello comes in to see what is happening. Iago renews his apparent efforts to stop the fight. Othello threatens the brawlers with punishment of death, and orders Iago to tell him how the fight began. "Honest Iago, who looks't dead with grieving," but who is secretly delighted with the success of his plans, tells the story so that it appears true to outward appearance; naturally, he does not disclose his own part in the affair. According to his account, one moment all was friendliness—the next, the participants were fighting like madmen. Othello turns to Cassio for an explanation; he is ashamed and cannot give any account—"I pray you, pardon me; I cannot speak." Othello then asks Montano, a man of grave and wise reputation. Montano however is wounded; moreover, he knows no reason why he should have been attacked; his only part in the brawl was self-defence.

Othello begins to lose his usual calm—"My blood begins my safer guides to rule." He insists upon knowing how it all began—such a quarrel, in a town still feeling the effects of the recent war, is disgraceful — particularly taking place amongst those whose duty it was to keep watch. Again he appeals to Iago. Montano also urges him to speak out.

Protesting that he would rather have his tongue cut out than use it to harm Cassio, Iago cunningly describes the affair to show Cassio in the worst possible light. He tells how the lieutenant burst in pursuing someone; how Montano stepped in to interfere and how he, Iago, followed this fellow to prevent his cries from alarming the town; during his brief absence Cassio and Montano had engaged in a sword fight, just as when Othello himself came in and found them. Iago knows that Cassio's disgrace and downfall are now sure; he indulges in a false defence of the lieutenant—"Yet surely Cassio, I believed, received From him that fled (Roderigo) some strange indignity Which patience could not pass."

Othello, completely deceived, answers that he knows Iago is trying to cover up Cassio's wrong-doing — "Thy honesty and love doth mince this matter, Making it light to Cassio." Regretfully, he dismisses Cassio from his rank. "Cassio, I love thee; But never more be officer of mine."

Desdemona, also aroused by the noise, enters. Othello's anger is increased to think that she has been disturbed. He leads her away, along with the wounded Montano, leaving Iago to quiet the town again.

Iago is left alone with Cassio; he enjoys himself thoroughly in his own fashion. Seemingly concerned, he inquires "What, are you hurt, lieutenant?" — gloating over the fact that Cassio is no longer a lieutenant. Cassio cares nothing for his wounds; it is his reputation that he mourns. His misfortune has sobered him. Iago makes light of his grief. "Reputation is an idle and most false imposition; oft got without merit, and lost without deserving." He assures Cassio that he can easily change Othello's mind. Cassio at first pays no attention but continues to berate himself for failing in his duty to so good a commander as Othello. Iago here slyly makes sure that Cassio did not know Roderigo — "What was he that you followed with your sword? What had he done to you?" Cassio cannot remember anything distinctly and continues to rail against his own folly in drinking.

Iago encourages him — "You or any man living may be drunk at a time, man." He then goes on to suggest to Cassio that Desdemona's influence is great with Othello; let Cassio beg her help in trying to persuade Othello to be lenient and give Cassio his place again. Cassio, ignorant of the evil schemes in Iago's head, is pleased with his advice. "You advise me well." He willingly agrees to approach Desdemona on the subject in the morning, and gratefully leaves Iago.

Iago is left alone to enjoy his success and look forward with vicious pleasure to further intrigues. He congratulates himself on the outward honesty of his advice. "And what's he then that says I play the villain? When this advice is free I give and honest, Probal to thinking and indeed the course To win the Moor again?" It is true that Othello is so in love with Desdemona that he will do anything she wishes—"How am I then a villain To counsel Cassio to this parallel course, Directly to his good?" In a paroxysm of delight at his own wickedness, he exclaims "Divinity of hell!"—planning to fill Othello's mind with suspicion of Cassio when he shall ask Desdemona to help him. By now Iago discloses the fact that he enjoys committing evil simply for its own sake—he has no particular quarrel with Desdemona, but "So will I turn her virtue into pitch, And out of her own goodness make the net That shall enmesh them all."

Roderigo comes in, complaining that nothing is turning out well for him; his money is almost spent; he has been beaten soundly, and threatens to profit by his experiences and return to Venice. This does not suit Iago. He counsels patience and points out that although Roderigo has had a beating, Cassio has suffered much more—he is cashiered, dismissed. Taking it for granted that Roderigo will obey him, he orders him to go to his dwelling and wait for him. The night has passed quickly and pleasantly for Iago—"By the mass, 'tis morning; Pleasure and action make the hours seem short."

Before leaving, he plans two more details—his wife Emilia must be told to speak in Cassio's favor to Desdemona; and he himself must contrive to have Othello see Cassio pleading with Desdemona to help him.

Commentary

As he promised, Othello is not allowing the celebration of his marriage to interfere with his duty—saying to Cassio "Let's teach ourselves that honourable stop, Not to outsport discretion." Still he has perfect trust in Iago—"Iago is most honest." Later, when the quarrel stirred up by Iago takes place, Othello's calm begins to give way to stern anger; his sense of authority and responsibility is shocked by such a brawl occurring amongst the watch, at a time when the townspeople most need reassurance after the Turkish threat of invasion. He demands to be told the whole story of the quarrel; he threatens to punish the one who began it to the limit. His belief in Iago is unshaken—he accepts his story of the affair without question. And although Cassio is dear to him, his stern sense of duty allows him no alternative—he dismisses the lieutenant without hesitation.

Cassio's too easy good-nature is his undoing in this scene. He cannot say "No" to Iago's seemingly friendly and generous offer of a "stoup of wine." Although he knows that he has had enough, and that he has not a head that can stand drinking, he protests too faintly and brings about his own downfall. "I'll do't; but it dislikes me." His good nature and desire to be a good companion outweigh his better judgment. His conscience troubles him nevertheless; he tries to believe that he has not had too much and that he can still attend to his duty—"Do not think, gentlemen, I am drunk . . ." He is quite right about his inability to hold much liquor—it immediately makes him quarrelsome, quick-tempered and unable to control himself—and Iago has the satisfaction of seeing his schemes work out perfectly.

Roderigo's obstinacy in continuing to hope that Iago may win Desdemona for him plays its part in the development of the plot. His stupidity in failing to realize that his suit will never be successful; his readiness to give Iago unlimited money, combined with his occasional burst of impatience at the failure of his desires, all serve to spur Iago on to further villainy in order to keep the dupe's money at his disposal.

Making the most of every opportunity in this scene, Iago skillfully plays several parts—the jolly companion of Cassio; the wise, regretful friend to Montano, falsely lamenting Cassio's weakness so that Montano will be the more impressed by it. His masterly description of the quarrel to Othello, which strengthens Othello's opinion of his honesty and friendliness toward Cassio, even while he is secretly exulting in his downfall, is the climax of his plans up till now. Again he skillfully shows great outward sympathy to Cassio, and gains the credit of suggesting a way of winning Othello's favor again—but a way which will involve the unfortunate Cassio in still deeper trouble.

His soliloquies show us his real thoughts; he is delighted with his success so far, and encouraged to go further and to involve even Desdemona, with whom he has no quarrel, in his unholy plots.

Notes

1. We are reminded that Roderigo, although not an important character in his own person, is the means of developing certain parts of the plot. As it was his dissatisfaction with Iago's help in courting Desdemona in the first place, now again his impatience spurs Iago on to further wickedness, in order to keep control of the young fool's money; we are given a hint of this here.

2. We are shown Othello's regard and affection for Cassio in the first lines of this scene—his dismissal comes as a dramatic contrast.

3. Othello, who up till now has shown only calm and self-control, begins to exhibit some of the force with which he acts later in the drama when Iago's poison has begun to work upon his mind—"Now, by heaven, My blood begins my safer guides to rule; And passion, having my best judgment collied, Assays to lead the way. If I once stir, Or do but lift this arm, the best of you Shall sink in my rebuke."

4. Iago's duplicity is exhibited to the full in this scene, where he gives an account of the quarrel which keeps to the truth only enough to make it sound plausible and at the same time manages to show up Cassio in the worst possible light to Othello, while appearing to try to protect the lieutenant.

5. Iago's wickedness advances rapidly at the end of the scene — up till now he has been able to provide a reasonable excuse to others and to himself for the evil deeds he is doing; now he openly acknowledges that he is contemplating evil for its own sake—he has no reason to hate Desdemona, but "So will I turn her virtue into pitch, And out of her own goodness make the net That shall enmesh them all."

ACT III · SCENE 1

Summary

There is a short interlude of relief and relaxation from the high tension, as Cassio introduces some musicians to play before the castle the next morning. There is usually a clown in Shakespeare's plays; here one appears for a very brief time. Evidently Othello does not care for the music and has sent the clown out to dismiss them. Cassio also uses him as a messenger, asking him to send Emilia, Iago's wife and Desdemona's attendant, out to speak with him.

Cassio's spirits are high now; when Iago enters, he finds that the lieutenant has already acted upon the suggestions of the night before. Here, as often, fate seems to play into Iago's hands — he does not need to pursuade Emilia to add her pleading to that of Cassio for

42

Desdemona's assistance, for Cassio has taken steps for that already.

Iago makes a lying promise to Cassio "I'll devise a means to draw the Moor Out of the way, that your converse and business May be more free." What he will really do is contrive to have Othello watch their conversation — read Act III, Scene 3, line 35 and following, where he begins to make insinuations to Othello about Cassio's behavior.

Emilia comes in to speak to Cassio, expressing her regret for his trouble. She tells him something that would save him further complications if he would only heed it — that Othello has said that his own regard for Cassio is the strongest factor in his treatment of him. Montano, whom Casssio wounded, is of such importance that the affair cannot be ignored, but there is hope for Cassio — Othello "protests he loves you and needs no other suitor but his likings To take the safest occasion by the front To bring you in again." If Cassio had not been too eager to take this as sufficient encouragement, and had decided not to ask Desdemona's help, Iago's plans would have been upset for the time being, although no doubt he would have made others. But he ignores this encouraging message which Emilia gives him, and proceeds with the original plan which Iago has suggested—"Yet, I beseech you, If you think fit, or that it may be done, Give me advantage of some brief discourse With Desdemona alone." So he unknowingly speeds on Iago's plots.

Commentary

The clown's few remarks to the musicians at the opening of the scene provide some relief from the tension which has been steadily mounting. Further, as little scenery was used on Elizabethan stages, Shakespeare used intervals such as this to indicate the time and place of the new action.

Although Othello does not appear in this scene, Emilia's account of his conversation with Desdemona about Cassio reveals his mental attitude towards the case—when he actually saw the quarrel taking place, he followed his impulse and dismissed Cassio upon the spot; now he has had time to judge the affair with less excitement, and has considered both sides of the question, Montano's position on the one hand, and his own regard for Cassio on the other. In the former scene as he says — "My blood begins my safer guides to rule" — in this scene his "safer guides," according to Emilia's account, are uppermost once more.

Notes

1. Cassio's impatience to follow Iago's advice is displayed—on his own initiative he decides to enlist Emilia's help also, so that she too is drawn into the plot.

2. There is plenty of dramatic irony in the fact that, as Emilia tells Cassio, Othello himself is ready to forgive Cassio when a suitable

opportunity arises; if Cassio were only content with this reassurance, there would be at least a delay in Iago's plans.

3. Suspense is created by Emilia's promise that she will make an opportunity for Cassio to speak to Desdemona alone; knowing Iago's preparations for such an occasion, the audience is brought to a high peak of anticipation.

4. Throughout the play there are innumerable references to Iago's "honesty." The irony of this serves to remind us that Iago is seldom what he appears to be.

ACT III · SCENE 2

Summary
This brief scene of a few lines shows us Iago taking a message from Othello to the pilot, and agreeing to meet his general later on the fortifications.

Commentary
With Cassio's dismissal, Iago is now closer to the general and will have more opportunity of working upon his feelings. Dramatically, the scene produces suspense by the knowledge that Othello and Iago are to meet later — Iago will use this as a means of having Othello come upon Cassio and Desdemona as they speak together.

ACT III · SCENE 3

Summary
There is a sharp break in the progress of the play in this scene at line 34, where Iago begins to work directly upon Othello's emotions — exclaiming "Ha! I like not that!" as they find Desdemona and Cassio together.

The scene takes place in the garden of the castle. Desdemona and Cassio enter, evidently ending an interview in which Cassio has asked for her help in persuading Othello to reinstate him and she has promised to do so. Emilia is with them and evidently believes that her husband Iago is also concerned about Cassio's disgrace. Desdemona assures Cassio that Othello thinks well of him and that his petition will be successful; Cassio is only afraid that when he is no longer in touch with Othello, the general may forget his former good record. Desdemona reassures him and promises to keep Cassio continually in Othello's mind — "I'll intermingle everything he does With Cassio's suit."

Emilia tells them that Othello is approaching. Although Desdemona urges Cassio to stay and hear how she will keep her promise, Cassio is still ashamed of his conduct of the night before, and hurries away. This action on his part gives Iago the very opportunity he wants, and he is quick to seize it.

Othello is completely unsuspicious. He is not jealous by nature, and Iago must put forth every effort to rouse even curiosity and the slightest uneasiness in his mind, at first. He has been thinking about Cassio, regretting the necessity of dismissing him, and any thoughts he has about him at the moment are not suspicious thoughts about his friendship with Desdemona, but regrets that he must still treat him with severity for his conduct.

Iago immediately begins to make insinuations against Cassio. "I cannot think it, That he would steal away so guilty-like, Seeing you coming" cleverly translating Cassio's shame at his foolish conduct into guilt at being found talking to Othello's wife. Othello, his mind still upon Cassio's drunken folly, does not yet grasp Iago's meaning. Desdemona, too, has no idea of the thoughts in Iago's mind and no intention of concealing the fact that she and Cassio have been together, but immediately tells Othello, and goes on to beg him to call Cassio back and give him some encouragement. But Othello's mind seems to be upon other things; he does not wish to speak to Cassio yet—"Not now, sweet Desdemona; some other time." Desdemona, showing a certain lack of tact, persists in spite of his evident unwillingness—"Why, then, tomorrow night; or Tuesday morn; On Tuesday noon, or night; on Wednesday morn." As she continues, she makes a remark that gives Iago material for further mischief. When she says "What! Michael Cassio, That came a-wooing with you, . . ." it occurs to Iago that this circumstance may be used in his schemes. See line 94, where he cunningly reminds Othello that at that time Cassio had many opportunities to see Desdemona.

Othello, unwilling to refuse Desdemona anything, at last yields—"Let him come when he will; I will deny thee nothing." Satisfied, she leaves with Emilia, while Othello impetuously expresses his love for her—"Excellent wretch! Perdition catch my soul, But I do love thee! and when I love thee not, Chaos is come again"—a fine example of dramatic irony, for as yet he has no conception of the fact that that time is near at hand.

Alone with Othello, Iago makes the most of his opportunities. With diabolical cleverness, he begins to make Othello's own imagination set to work, by suggesting, by refusing to speak out, but continually planting seeds of curiosity and uneasiness in the general's mind. This indirect method finally results in rousing Othello to real curiosity as to Iago's thoughts. "What dost thou think?"

Iago, instead of making a direct accusation against Desdemona and Cassio, continues to hold back, to give the impression that he knows far more than he is saying. Othello is now completely alert. "By heaven, he echoes me, As if there were some monster in his thoughts Too hideous to be shown." He brings all Iago's remarks together and begins to see the picture that Iago is sketching; he demands to know what it means. Iago still evades the question, knowing that his hesitation will make Othello more eager to find out his thoughts. This has the desired effect; Othello exclaims that this broken interrupted speech of Iago shows great emotion; he is still convinced of Iago's honesty and says that he is incapable of speaking in this way merely to produce an effect; dishonest men could do so, but not Iago.

Iago proceeds carefully, still avoiding direct accusations against Cassio, but arousing Othello's suspicion by ambiguous remarks. "For Michael Cassio, I dare be sworn I *think* that he is honest . . . Men should be what they seem." Othello responds—"give thy worst of thoughts The worst of words."

Iago still refuses, implying that his thoughts are too vile to utter, and that they would be better left unsaid. "It were not for your quiet nor your good, Nor for my manhood, honesty, or wisdom, To let you know my thoughts." This reticence on his part, as he knows very well, makes Othello determined to know his meaning—"By heaven, I'll know thy thoughts." Instead of replying directly, Iago sanctimoniously warns Othello against the emotion of jealousy—thus putting the idea of jealousy into Othello's mind.

Even yet Othello does not grasp the idea that Iago is speaking of a definite case; he agrees that jealousy is an unworthy feeling and expresses his own freedom from it; he realizes Desdemona's accomplishments and popularity, but at the same time he is confident, for the reason that she chose him of her own free will. But, he says, if there is ever any question of doubt, he will require proof—"I'll see before I doubt; when I doubt, prove; And on the proof, there is more but this—Away at once with love or jealousy!"

Now Iago becomes more explicit. "I speak not yet of proof. Look against Desdemona's character, at the same time indirectly bringing up to your wife; observe her well with Cassio." He makes an insinuation that Othello is a foreigner—"I know our country disposition well; In Venice they do let heaven see the pranks They dare not show their husbands; their best conscience Is not to leave't undone, but keep't unknown." He follows this up with a sharper thrust—"She did deceive her father, marrying you; And when she seemd'd to shake and fear your looks, She loved them most."

At last Othello is moved. "And so she did." Iago sees that his poisonous words are beginning to have an effect, and knows better than to enlarge upon the ideas already planted in Othello's mind—Othello's own imagination will accomplish more. He pretends to regret what he has said—"but I am much to blame; I humbly do beseech you of your pardon For too much loving you." He protests that his words are not to be taken too seriously—"I am to pray you not to strain my speech To grosser issues nor to larger reach Than to suspicion." Pretending concern, he remarks "My lord, I see you're moved."

Othello refuses to let himself believe that Desdemona is to be suspected. "I do not think but Desdemona honest." Iago falsely agrees—"Long live she so! and long live you to think so!" But Othello is no longer quite sure—"And yet, how nature erring from itself—"

His doubts encourage Iago—and once more he comes into the open. Since Desdemona has shown a certain peculiarity in choosing Othello, the Moor, as a husband, instead of one of her own race and color, she may show unnatural tendencies in other directions. But having expressed this thought, Iago hastily retreats again, apologizing for such opinions.

The mischief is done; Othello descends to the shameful action of telling Iago to continue his tale-bearing about Desdemona, and even to set Emilia on the same course. He dismisses Iago, who goes, but returns immediately with a new suggestion. Let Othello put Cassio off for a while, before he consents to return him to favor. This, says Iago, will give Othello an opportunity to observe any particular effort on Desdemona's part to have Cassio forgiven for his behavior of the previous night. In the meantime, Iago urges with deceptive open-mindedness, let Othello believe that she is innocent. Having planted this new idea in his general's mind, Iago again leaves him.

Othello is left alone to think over what has been said. He is still sure of Iago's honesty, and of his knowledge of human nature. Usually Othello is not given to introspection and study of himself, but here he has been brought to an unusual state of mind and begins to look within for reasons for Desdemona's supposed faithlessness. "I am black, And have not those soft parts of conversation That chamberers have, or for I am declined Into the vale of years—" He is bewildered, full of humility, torn between his love for Desdemona and the horror he feels at the idea of her fault. When she enters with Emilia, he cannot bring himself to believe that the charge is true—"If she be false, O, then heaven mocks itself! I'll not believe't."

Now comes the incident of the handkerchief which the dramatist makes use of to bring about the final disaster. Desdemona, quite ignorant of what has been put in her husband's mind by Iago, enters to tell him that the islanders of Cyprus are waiting for him to come to a dinner which he has arranged. Othello answers faintly; he is still stunned by Iago's charges against her. In answer to her inquires he tells her that he has a headache. Desdemona tenderly offers to bind his forehead with her handkerchief; Othello puts it aside, saying that it is too small, and it drops to the ground. Without noticing it, they leave the garden.

Emilia, who entered with Desdemona, picks it up, exclaiming that it was Othello's first present to Desdemona. Iago, for some unknown reason, has already urged her to steal it for him, but Desdemona has always treasured it and kept it near her because Othello has told her to do so. Emila, not knowing what direful consequences her dishonest action will have, decides to copy the embroidery on the handkerchief and give it to Iago, simply to satisfy what she thinks is his whim.

Iago comes in, scolding Emilia, but she pacifies him by showing him the handkerchief. Iago snatches it from her in spite of Emilia's protests, and dismisses her.

This mere accident and freak of fortune has played into Iago's hands; he decides to "plant" the handkerchief in Cassio's lodging and let him find it there; mischief will surely follow. Iago exults to himself, realizing that Othello is already succumbing to his hints. As his General enters, he mutters to himself with cruel delight — "Not poppy, nor mandragora, Nor all the drowsy syrups of the world, Shall ever medicine thee to that sweet sleep Which thou owedst yesterday."

By now Othello is convinced that Iago's accusations are true. He laments that he knows the truth about her; he grieves that his honorable career is ended. Iago says little for the moment, letting Othello's distress have full play. The Moor appeals to Iago to bring him positive proof of Desdemona's infidelity; he may have a faint hope that it is not so; at any rate certainty will be better than uncertainty and the working of his imagination. He threatens Iago; the proof must be absolute—"or woe upon thy life!"

Iago breaks out into protestations—this is his reward for being honest! He vows that he will never show his friendship for anyone again by being honest with them—"from hence I'll love no friend, sith love breeds such offence."

Othello is taken in once more by his successful acting—"Nay, stay. Thou shouldst be honest." But his faith has been shaken in Desdemona; naturally it may also be shaken in Iago. Again he asks for definite proof.

Iago expresses false concern—"I see, sir, you are eaten up with passion. I do repent me that I put it to you." Then he tells an utterly false story, to the effect that he overheard Cassio talking in his sleep, evidently dreaming of making love to Desdemona. Iago protests, as if to try to reassure Othello, that of course it was only a dream, but Othello is affected. "I'll tear her all to pieces." Iago, still protesting that Desdemona may be honest, then uses his strongest piece of false evidence—the handkerchief. He tells Othello that he has seen Cassio using "a handkerchief spotted with strawberries" to wipe his beard—accurately describing the embroidery on the linen.

Othello is convinced now—"Now do I see 'tis true." He is determined to have revenge. Iago, sure that his work is accomplished, pretends to counsel patience. But Othello swears to be avenged. Iago, in blasphemous mockery, kneels with him, promising his help. Othello accepts his offer and orders him—"Within these three days let me hear thee say That Cassio's not alive." Iago consents, and to tempt Othello still further, recalls Desdemona to his mind "But let her live." It has the desired effect; Othello is resolved to kill her also—"I will withdraw, To furnish me with some swift means of death For the fair devil." Iago has a further triumph as the scene ends—"Now art thou my lieutenant."

Commentary

Emilia is innocent of any malice towards Desdemona and Othello; as yet she has no idea of Iago's plots against them and her part in the intrigue is played in ignorance of the schemes of her husband. "I warrant it grieves my husband as if the case were his." When she picks up the handkerchief, she only intends to copy the embroidery and give a similar one to Iago, who wishes it, as she believes, only for a whim. "I nothing but to please his fantasy." She is dismayed when Iago seizes it—"Give't me again. Poor lady, she'll run mad when she shall lack it." As yet she believes in her husband and does what he tells her without question.

Still filled with shame and regret for his folly of the night before, Cassio's self-consciousness moves him to retire as Othello enters, the action which Iago is quick to seize upon as evidence of a guilty conscience, and which gives him the opportunity of remarking upon it to Othello. Cassio is still unable to believe that Othello will forgive him of his own free will; it is his own impatience and eagerness to be reinstated in the general's favor that leads to his own undoing.

Iago's genius for evil is displayed to the full in this scene. He is quick to seize upon every chance occurrence that will further his ends. Cassio's disappearance at the sight of Othello is made the text of his insinuations. Iago realizes that he will accomplish more by seeming to hold back facts than by speaking out openly against Cassio; his hesitation arouses Othello's curiosity and interest; his half-truths and faltering answers stimulate Othello's own imagination far beyond anything that Iago could say directly. Very gradually and carefully he proceeds from this indirect method of accusation to more direct attack, when he sees that Othello has been worked up to a state of mind that will accept plainer speaking. "Now I shall have reason To show the love and duty that I bear you With franker spirit. . .Look to your wife." If Iago had spoken those words to Othello at the beginning of the interview, the General would never have listened; but Iago has played upon his feelings until his insinuations seem likely. Step by step Iago advances, always seeming to hold back, until Othello's better nature begins to crumble and he not only listens credulously to Iago but even asks him to keep watch on Desdemona. Iago does not give him time to consider his evidence calmly and coolly, but rapidly builds up a tissue of half-truth and lies that completely convince the Moor. Iago's heartless satisfaction breaks out in his aside—"Not poppy, nor mandragora, Nor all the drowsy syrups of the world, Shall ever medicine thee to that sweet sleep Which thou owedst yesterday." He displays cold-blooded, blasphemous humor in his oath to Othello, who is sincerely vowing a vengeance which he feels is righteous.

Sincerely concerned about Cassio, Desdemona knows that he is a worthy soldier and hardly deserves dismissal for one night's folly. She knows Othello's regard for him and feels sure that she will succeed in persuading her husband to take Cassio back. She is surprised that Othello delays in granting her request—it is not a test of his love for her, for it does not concern her personally at all.

The real tragedy begins here in Othello's own soul — he allows

Iago's accusations and insinuations against his wife and his friend to affect his own natural nobility of mind. He has no tendency towards jealousy; it takes all Iago's skill to bring the idea to his mind; he fights against it as long as he can, until Iago's seemingly overwhelming evidence makes him believe. This shows us how Iago's superior mind works on the lesser one of Othello. At every turn, Iago's answer is worse than the truth, for it drives Othello relentlessly forward, forcing him to pass from questioning to interrogation, from friend to detective, from a reasonable man to an unreasonable one. Few military minds live easily with any sort of frustration, and Othello is no exception. Finally, Othello's frustration blisters forth:

> Think my lord! By heaven, he echoes me,
> As if there were some monster in his thought
> Too hideous to be shown. Thou dost mean something:
> I heard thee say even now, thou likedst not that,
> When Cassio left my wife: what didst not like?
> And when I told thee he was of my counsel
> In my whole course of wooing, thou criedst "Indeed!"
> And didst contract and purse thy brow together,
> As if thou then hadst shut up in thy brain
> Some horrible conceit. If thou dost love me,
> Show me thy thought.   (lines 106-116)

Othello's reference to Iago's facial grimaces is one of Shakespeare's careful stage directions. When we picture as well as hear Iago, his evil suggestion is very convincing; Othello has good reason to be alarmed so easily when the agent of the alarm is as subtle and wickedly ingenious as Iago.

When Othello says that he considers Cassio an honest man, Iago agrees that he *thinks* so too, implying that he of course can not know this for a fact. Othello then says that "Men should be what they seem," which has become one of the major themes of the play. Othello's entire downfall will be caused by believing that what he sees is true. Because Othello is so easily deceived by appearances, he becomes a weaker prey in the hands of Iago. When Iago can show Desdemona and Cassio talking together in a secretive way, he can make it *seem* to Othello that his wife is unfaithful. And the turning point of the play is when Othello will see with his own eyes the proof of Desdemona's guilt. In other words, the entire play is an argument that things are *not* really what they seem. It never occurs to Othello that Iago could be his undoer or enemy, because Iago has always *seemed* such an honest man. Shakespeare has Othello point this out again and again in the first few acts of the play, suggesting to the audience that Othello makes certain assumptions about people which he never questions unless he sees some reason not to believe in them any longer.

Notes

1. Iago's diabolic cleverness and adroitness in using every possible means to bring about his desired results are displayed to the full in this temptation scene.

2. The beginning of Othello's fall is shown — he allows Iago's evil thoughts to enter his own mind, and the force of evil within himself conflicts with his natural virtue and begins to conquer it—the tragedy is the breaking down of his own moral character.

3. The episode of the handkerchief is the dramatist's device for precipitating the tragic events about to follow.

ACT III · SCENE 4

Summary

Before the castle, Desdemona is asking the clown to find Cassio and send him to her; she is sure that she has persuaded Othello to forgive him. Here is one example of dramatic irony—Othello, instead of being in a mood to forgive Cassio for his drunken folly, is ready to have him murdered for a supposed intrigue with Desdemona. Another example follows—Desdemona, worrying over the loss of the handkerchief, tells Emilia that the Moor is absolutely free from any suspicion or jealousy—otherwise he might misconstrue the loss of the handkerchief. "My noble Moor Is true of mind and made of no such baseness As jealous creatures are. . .I think the sun where he was born Drew all such humours from him." Although it is true that Othello is naturally free from such feelings, by now he has been worked up to such a pitch of suspicion by Iago that he is ready to believe anything of Desdemona.

Othello enters; taking Desdemona's hand, he expresses his divided feelings—he still loves her, yet hates the sin of which he believes her guilty. Desdemona does not understand and ignores his feverish talk, telling him that she has sent for Cassio to speak with the Moor. Othello, in turn ignoring what she has said, pretends that he needs a handkerchief and asks for hers—the "strawberry-spotted" one which he believes she has given Cassio. Desdemona replies that she has not got it with her. Othello tells her the history of it. An Egyptian charmer gave it to his mother, telling her that it had power to keep her husband's love; if she lost it, he would feel not love but loathing for her. Othello's mother, when she was dying, gave it to Othello, telling him to give it to his own wife. Othello warns Desdemona that its loss will mean disaster. Desdemona is terrified, as Othello elaborates upon its magical qualities—"there's magic in the web of it."

When Othello asks her directly if it is lost, she prevaricates and tries to evade his questioning. Othello demands to see it. Desdemona, with dignity, replies that she can produce it, but refuses to do so immediately, accusing Othello of using this matter as a pretext for putting off Cassio's suit. Othello, his anger increasing, continually demands the handkerchief and finally losing all self-control—"Away!" leaves her wondering and dismayed, completely at a loss as to the cause of his anger.

Cassio and Iago enter. The former, encouraged by Iago, again importunes Desdemona to use her influence with Othello. When Desdemona tells him that Othello does not seem to be himself, that it is useless to plead with him, Iago is secretly delighted. "Is my lord angry?" He must see the effect he has had upon Othello. "I will go meet him." He is pleased that he has stirred Othello's usual calm. "Can he be angry? . . . There's matter in't indeed, if he be angry."

Desdemona expresses her conjectures as to the reasons for Othello's disturbed state of mind — matters of state, either from Venice or in the Island of Cyprus. She is reasonable and sensible — she realizes that when men are disturbed about important affairs, they are apt to be short-tempered about trivialities. "Men's natures wrangle with inferior things, Though great ones are their object." Emilia, on the other hand, hopes that this is true, rather than what she suspects — that he is jealous of Desdemona for some unknown reason. Desdemona is still sure that Othello is incapable of this — "Heaven keep that monster from Othello's mind!" The women leave Cassio alone; he is joined by Bianca, his mistress.

Bianca reproaches him for staying away from her so long. He apologizes, telling her that he has been in trouble. He gives her Desdemona's handkerchief, (which Iago has put in his lodging) asking her to take out the embroidery. Bianca is immediately jealous, thinking that some other woman has given it to him. This is ordinary jealousy, contrasted with Othello's reluctant and unwilling belief in Desdemona's guilt.

Cassio denies her accusations, telling her that he found the handkerchief in his room. He asks her to leave him, for he feels that his coming interview with Othello will not be improved if the general finds a woman with him. He promises to see her again soon, and they leave together.

Commentary

The clown is simply a clown, typical of his kind, without any particular characteristics; he provides a small amount of comic relief and serves as a messenger from Desdemona to Cassio—to carry an innocent message but one which might be misconstrued and used by Iago as something sinister.

Emilia is deceitful here—when Desdemona asks her where she may have lost the handkerchief, Emilia answers that she does not know. Still it is with no idea of harming Desdemona—simply to please her husband Iago's fancy for the handkerchief. She has a poor idea of men; she takes it for granted that Othello is probably jealous, and her philosophy is that men consider that women are only created for their pleasure.

Desdemona is entirely lacking in suspicion of any evil. Her mind is still full of Cassio's trouble. In her innocence she is still little concerned with the loss of the handkerchief, sure that her husband would never let jealousy enter his mind. She is at a loss to understand Othello's strange demeanor. His evident excitement about the handkerchief disturbs her, but it is wonder, not guilt, that she feels. She is unwise in putting off his questions, instead of confessing that she has lost it, but still she does not realize what is behind it all. Unsuspicious, she accuses Othello of bringing up the question in order to take her mind from Cassio, little realizing that to Othello, by this time, the mention of Cassio's name is shameless and brazen impudence. She is completely in the dark with regard to Othello's behavior, and assigns it to his concentration upon matters of state.

Although Othello's behavior mystifies Desdemona, it is clear to the reader that he is suffering the tortures of two opposite passions—his love for Desdemona and his belief in her guilt. Usually transparent and open, he descends here to a slight deceit in order to bring up the question of the handkerchief—"I have a salt and sorry rheum offends me; Lend me thy handkerchief." When he first courted Desdemona, his imaginative and descriptive powers stood him in good stead; here again he displays them powerfully in his account of the history of the magical handkerchief. His self-control is decreasing; her continual evasion and repeated references to Cassio are too much for him, and he leaves Desdemona in anger.

Cassio is as impatient as ever—"I would not be delayed." We see a new side of his character upon Bianca's entrance. It is rather interesting to note that Cassio is much more gentle and polite to Bianca, a woman of doubtful reputation, than Iago is to his own wife Emilia.

The plotter, Iago, is pleased with his success so far—"Is my lord angry?" expresses his secret delight in the fact. He gloats over the fact—dwelling on Othello's calm in critical moments, and rejoicing that something has shaken it at last—"There's matter in't indeed, if he be angry." His hearers are unconscious of his elation; only the reader, or the audience, knows what is behind his words.

Bianca is to be used later as another instrument of Iago's schemes; here her petty jealousy, of the most ordinary and trivial nature, aroused by a trifle, is a contrast to the deep passion of suspicion which has with difficulty been stirred up in Othello by Iago.

Notes

1. This scene increases the feeling of tension and sense of tragedy to come, filled as it is with dramatic irony. Desdemona is sure that she has persuaded Othello to look favorably upon Cassio again, while the Moor is in reality seething with jealous rage against him. Again, Desdemona is confident that her husband has no jealousy in his nature; he has not, until now, when Iago has produced that feeling in him.

2. The discussion about the handkerchief leads the reader to believe that perhaps it may not play an important part in the tragedy after all;

there is still a chance that it may be returned to Desdemona before the mischief is done. The tension is thus still further heightened.

3. Most importantly, this scene pictures the struggle taking place in Othello's mind between his love for Desdemona and his hate for the guilt of which he believes her capable; again there is suspense as the reader wonders which feeling will triumph.

ACT IV · SCENE 1

Summary

Before the castle, Iago and Othello are in the midst of a conversation in which Iago is persistently keeping the idea of jealousy in Othello's mind. Pretending to think that there may be nothing wrong between people who are discovered kissing each other, he inflames Othello's imagination and increases the torture in the General's mind. Othello protests that a kiss should not be given lightly; Iago makes nothing of that—"So they do nothing, 'tis a venial slip"—but goes on to remind him of the incident of the handkerchief—a visible evidence of some intrigue. Othello has been trying to forget it—but Iago's remarks bring it back to him—"O, it comes o'er my memory, As doth the raven over the infected house, Boding to all—he had my handkerchief." Then Iago brings a further pressure to bear upon Othello; leading him to believe that Cassio has actually boasted of his love affair with Desdemona. Othello, overcome by his emotions, breaks into a confused outburst of words — "What? what? . . . Handkerchief — confessions — handkerchief!" and falls in a trance at the feet of Iago, who exults over his senseless body — "Work on, My medicine, work! . . ."

Cassio enters and wishes to try to revive him. But Iago already has another plan working in his mind. Explaining that the attack must run its course, he tells Cassio to retire now and return when Othello has recovered and gone away. Unsuspecting, Cassio obeys.

Othello returns to consciousness, his mind still filled with Iago's false accusations against Cassio and Desdemona. "Did he confess it?" Iago advises him to accept the fact—Othello is not the only man whose wife is unfaithful to him. Then, in order that Othello may be convinced, he advises him to hide himself where he can hear Cassio boasting to Iago of his conquest of Desdemona—"For I will make him tell the tale anew."

Othello consents to take part in this degrading scheme and hides to overhear the conversation between Iago and Cassio, who enters immediately.

Iago, in a short speech while he is alone before Cassio enters, explains that he is going to contrive to have Cassio speak slightingly of his mistress Bianca—Othello is to believe that he is speaking of Desdemona, and — "As he shall smile, Othello shall go mad; And his unbookish jealousy must construe Poor Cassio's smiles, gestures and light behaviour, Quite in the wrong."

He greets Cassio sardonically — "How do you now, lieutenant" — knowing that the title, which Cassio has lost, will wound his feelings, and remind him of the loss of his rank. However, as if to comfort him, he advises to continue his pleading with Desdemona to influence Othello to restore him to favor. Othello hears him speak of Desdemona, and just as Iago has schemed, believes that the ensuing conversation is about her. Iago, however, in a lower tone, which Othello cannot hear, leads Cassio to talk about Bianca—"Now, if this suit lay in Bianca's power, How quickly should you speed!"

Cassio, unsuspecting, falls into the trap and discusses Bianca freely. "Alas, poor rogue! I think, i'faith, she loves me." Othello is worked up to a fury of jealous rage, believing that all Cassio's references to Bianca are spoken about Desdemona. "She was here even now; she haunts me in every place. I was the other day talking on the sea-bank with certain Venetians; and thither comes the bauble, and, by this hand, she falls me thus about my neck—"

By a stroke of fortune which seems to attend Iago's evil plans, Bianca herself comes in at this moment. This might upset another person; Iago, however, is quick to take advantage of it for his own ends. And Bianca's first words must seem to Othello, listening, a confirmation of Iago's stories—"What did you mean by that same handkerchief you gave me even now?. . .This is some minx's token. . ."

This is the climax of the play; Othello sees the handkerchief in the hands of Bianca. This also marks the beginning of the third stage of the drama—the results of the conflict—the conclusion or catastrophe.

By now Othello must be convinced that Desdemona has given the handkerchief to Cassio, who thinks so lightly of her that he has passed it on to his mistress. Bianca leaves, in a temper, but telling Cassio that he may come to supper with her to explain matters. Iago urges him to follow her, and is left with Othello, who has been completely convinced by the foregoing interview between Iago and Cassio, and is determined to kill the latter. "How shall I murder him, Iago?" Iago, not satisfied with his success, tantalizes him still further—"Did you perceive how he laughed at his vice. . .And did you see the handkerchief. . .and to see how he prizes the foolish woman your wife! she gave it to him, and he hath given it his whore."

Othello is in mental agony, at one moment recalling Desdemona's loveliness, the next, suffering anguish at the thought of her supposed wickedness—"O Iago, the pity of it, Iago!" He determines to poison her, without giving her a chance to make him relent—"I'll not expostulate with her, lest her body and beauty unprovide my mind again. This night, Iago." Iago, still unsatisfied, and grown quite bold with his success so far, urges worse punishment—"strangle her in her bed." Othello accepts the suggestion. Iago promises to deal with Cassio. A trumpet call interrupts them.

Desdemona enters, accompanied by attendants and by Lodovico, a kinsman of her father Brabantio, from Venice. He brings a letter to Othello from the Duke and senators of that city. While Othello reads it, Desdemona tells Lodovico of the trouble between her husband and Cassio — not of course the one invented by Iago of which she knows nothing, but Cassio's dismissal for drunkenness and fighting. Although Othello appears to be reading the letter from Venice, his mind is upon Desdemona and her words about Cassio, and mutters comments which the others cannot interpret rightly — "Fire and brimstone!" At first they think that the contents of the letter from Venice have made him angry; suddenly he strikes Desdemona. Lodovico is horrified "My lord, this would not be believed in Venice, Though I should swear I saw't. 'Tis very much. Make her amends; she weeps." But Othello thrusts her away — "Out of my sight!" and she obediently leaves. Lodovico is concerned and begs Othello to call her back. Othello takes the opportunity to insult her and put her to shame before her old friends; he calls her, taunts her with her obedience, and dismisses her again.

The letter from Venice contains a command for Othello to return there. He announces this, invites Lodovico to supper, and leaves with a confused mutter "Goats and monkeys," referring to something which has a meaning for him, but not for the others.

Lodovico, left with Iago, expresses his shocked astonishment in the change in Othello; Iago strengthens this impression "He is much changed . . . Alas, alas! It is not honesty in me to speak What I have seen and known . . . Do but go after, And mark how he continues." Lodovico, convinced that Othello is out of his mind, follows to watch him.

Commentary

In this scene Othello is attempting a real investigation, but he is too blinded by jealousy and anger to understand what he sees, and to realize that Iago has manipulated him.

Triumph for Iago is complete in this scene; his power over Othello is assured, and his enjoyment in the situation is at its height. He is safe in speaking openly and insultingly of Desdemona, and does not hesitate to suggest means of revenge to Othello. Everything appears to be working in his favor — Bianca's appearance affords him a further line to follow; Lodovico sees Othello strike Desdemona and is easily convinced that he has been acting strangely for some time. As Othello was at his happiest in Act II Scene 1, where he rejoins Desdemona in Cyprus, so here Iago revelling in the success of all his schemes; nothing seems to stand in his way.

As a contrast to this, Othello's nature is disintegrating; Iago's proofs convince him beyond doubt of Desdemona's faithlessness; his mind is temporarily affected with rage and grief. After a period of unconsciousness he wakes to obey every suggestion of Iago, to believe all that is told and shown to him, and plan instant punishment for Cassio and Desdemona.

With his playful, mocking talk of Bianca, Cassio is the unwitting instrument in Iago's hands; his good nature prevails when Bianca scolds him.

Desdemona is puzzled by Othello's behavior, grieved and shocked by his brutal treatment, docile and anxious to please him, with no thought of resenting or retaliating; she is stunned, completely in the dark as to the reason for his actions and words.

Lodovico is used to represent the reaction of the average person upon seeing Othello's behavior — he is shocked and dismayed. Also, he is used by Iago as a means to spread the news of Othello's seeming madness.

Notes

1. This scene shows Iago at the height of his power over Othello. He has reduced the Moor to such a state that his noble nature has given way to confusion, suspicion and finally certainty of Desdemona's guilt; Iago no longer needs to proceed cautiously and subtly, but speaks openly in disparagement of Desdemona and finally suggests to Othello the means of her death. Iago's power is at its peak; Othello has reached the lowest depths.

2. Iago's plan to have Othello overhear Cassio speaking of Bianca (or as Othello believes, Desdemona) makes it plausible for the Moor to demand revenge against Cassio, and to punish Desdemona for her breach of faith. Bianca's entrance, carrying the handkerchief, also gives him what appears to be concrete evidence of the truth of the story. Up until now, all the evidence has been hearsay; now, with these events, Othello is convinced for himself.

3. This scene contains a major turning point in the drama—the climax. Up to now we have had the introduction or exposition, and the complications or conflict in which the action rises. Here the climax occurs, when Othello sees Bianca with the handkerchief. From this point on, the consequences of Iago's plotting take place, and the events produce their own results.

4. Bianca's invitation to Cassio for supper gives Iago another advantage; later, when Cassio is stabbed, he turns suspicion against Bianca (Act V, Scene 1) — "Prithee, Emilia, Go know of Cassio where he supp'd to-night" — implying that Bianca has attacked him.

5. Lodovico's arrival concerning matters of state relieves the tension only momentarily; it marks a contrast between Desdemona's pleasure in seeing a friend from her home, and the fate that is in store for her. Othello's reception of the visitor recalls him for a moment to his former sense of responsibility and adds still another element to the struggle which is going on within him.

ACT IV · SCENE 2

Summary

In the first part of this scene, Othello refuses to believe Emilia's protestations that her mistress Desdemona is innocent. Then follows a dramatic interview between Othello and Desdemona in which he accuses her outright of being a woman of bad character. The scene ends with Roderigo turning upon Iago for failing to keep his promises with regard to Desdemona—a hint that Iago himself may become involved in the complex plot he has woven about the others.

In a room in the castle, Emilia is protesting to Othello that she has never seen Desdemona behaving in any way unbecomingly with Cassio, although she has been present at many of their interviews. Othello tries to refresh her memory—"What, did they never whisper?. . .Nor send you out o' the way. . .To fetch her fan, her gloves, her mask, nor nothing?" Emilia is firm, and insists that Desdemona is honest—with dramatic irony she abuses the wretch who has put suspicion into Othello's head, never dreaming that the wretch is her own husband. Othello would be glad to believe her, but Iago's poisonous suggestions have become too firmly implanted in his mind; he does not respect Emilia enough to believe that she is speaking the truth, but suspects that she is merely shielding Desdemona.

He orders Emilia to bring Desdemona to him, then proceeds to play out a revolting scene in which he makes it appear that Desdemona is entertaining him as though he were one of her lovers, while Emilia is set to watch outside the door to keep their interview secret. Desdemona kneels before him, begging him to explain his inexplicable fury against her. He commands her to swear that she is loyal to him; for to him she is still so angelic that unless she perjures herself by taking a false oath, "the devils themselves Should fear to seize her."

Desdemona, in perfect faith, swears that she is true. This resolves the question in Othello's mind. Since she has, as he believes, sworn a false oath, he feels justified now in his decision to kill her. But he weeps, and Desdemona asks the reason, thinking perhaps that his grief comes from his recall from Cyprus, and that he blames her father for the order.

Othello breaks out into lamentations; he protests that he could have borne any affliction—shame, poverty, imprisonment, even ridicule; but to lose the treasure of his love, on which his whole life depends, is unendurable. Desdemona protests her innocence; she asks what sin she has committed. He accuses her, at the same time tortured by the thought of her beauty. "O thou weed, Who art so lovely fair and smells't so sweet That the sense aches at thee, would thou hadst ne'er been born!" In spite of her protestations he refuses to believe her, contemptuously calls Emilia and flings her money, and leaves her with her mistress.

Desdemona is stunned by Othello's treatment; she answers Emilia's questions dazedly and asks her to bring Iago. She implores of him, of all people, to intercede for her, thereby giving him an opportunity to gloat in secret over the misery he has caused. Iago, of course, pretends ignorance and gives himself the additional enjoyment of hearing the story from Emilia. She is filled with indignation against the person who has poisoned the Moor's mind—"A halter pardon him! and hell gnaw his bones!" Iago hushes her abusive language, taking a grim private pleasure from the fact that she is referring to himself. Desdemona, again on her knees, begs Iago to speak to Othello in her behalf, swearing her faithfulness and her undying love for her husband, in spite of his unkindness.

Roderigo enters as the women leave, and shows unusual spirit in accusing Iago of procrastinating—"Every day thou daffest me with some device." He has come to the end of his patience. "I will indeed no longer endure it." Iago, full of triumph over Desdemona's easy submission to him, at first makes little effort to placate him. Roderigo becomes more excited as he recites the wrongs Iago has done him; he suspects that the jewels he gave Iago as bribes to Desdemona have not found their way to her; certainly she has shown Roderigo no signs of "sudden respect and acquaintance." At last he makes an open threat—"I will make myself known to Desdemona. If she will return me my jewels, I will give over my suit and repent my unlawful solicitation; if not, assure yourself I will seek satisfaction of you."

Iago's retort is short, but full of direful meaning "You have said now"—in other words, you have pronounced your own death sentence by those words. However, he begins to use the methods by which he usually persuades the dupe, flattering him and assuring him that although results are not visible as yet, he is sure of winning Desdemona. To excite him further, he tells the dupe that Cassio is to take Othello's place in Cyprus, while the Moor is to leave for Mauritania with Desdemona. However, if Roderigo is daring enough to kill Cassio, Othello and Desdemona will have to stay in Cyprus, and Roderigo's hopes may be realized. So Iago hopes literally to kill two birds with one stone and get rid of both Cassio and Roderigo, who is becoming too demanding. Roderigo is still doubtful — "I will hear further reason for this" — but as may be expected, he is about to yield once more to Iago's persuasiveness.

Commentary

Emilia's importance in the plot is increasing. Her indignation against the person who has lied about Desdemona prepares the way for her denunciation of Iago later on. Although she is not a completely admirable character, she is devoted and loyal to her mistress.

Here Othello is acting according to his beliefs and principles; he has been convinced beyond a doubt by Iago that Desdemona has been false to him, and although it causes him anguish, it is his conviction that he must pronounce her death sentence. His own life is ruined — "But there, where I have garner'd up my heart, Where either I must live, or bear no life; The fountain from the which my current runs, Or else dries up; to be discarded thence!'' The scorn and bitterness with which he treats Desdemona come from his grief.

In her innocence, Desdemona is completely bewildered by her husband's charges. Even the words he uses are a shock to her delicacy and dignity. Still she has no feeling of resentment or reproach against him—''Unkindness may do much; And his unkindness may defeat my life, But never taint my love.'' Her appeal to Iago, the cause of her misery, is pitiful in the extreme.

Roderigo begins to show some strength of character in his revolt against Iago. His independence and new unwillingness to accept all Iago's suggestions are the beginning of the turn of fortune against Iago.

The pretended words of comfort to Desdemona emphasize Iago's despicable character. He is impatient and casual with Emilia, not realizing the depth of her resentment against the slander of Desdemona. He is still confident of his power over Roderigo, in spite of the young man's objections—''I will show you such a necessity in his death that you shall think yourself bound to put it on him . . . About it.'' His confidence is producing a carelessness which foretells his downfall.

Notes

1. In this scene Othello believes that he justifies himself for the murder of Desdemona. He is going to kill her, not in jealous rage, but because he believes that she is lying when she swears that she is true to him; therefore, the murder will be justifiable punishment.

2. Emilia's indignation against the unknown slanderer of Desdemona is increasing; it is dramatically worked up to the point where later she turns upon Iago and exposes him as the villain.

3. Desdemona's appeal to Iago to help her is the height of irony; it raises him to a point from which his later fall will be all the greater.

4. Roderigo's rebellion against Iago prepares us for the coming downfall of the villain.

5. A further complication is introduced by Iago's plan to have Roderigo attack Cassio, hoping to dispose of the two at once.

ACT IV · SCENE 3

Summary

This pathetic picture of Desdemona, a period of comparative calm between the dramatic events preceding it and the emotional tension of the last act, gives a breathing space, and yet increases the suspense rather than gives a relief to the spectator.

The company are returning from supper. Othello is about to walk with Lodovico, and curtly orders Desdemona to go to bed and dismiss

Emilia. Emilia is surprised, but Desdemona's only desire is to obey him. As Emilia helps her to undress, Desdemona dwells upon her love for Othello—even "his checks, his frowns . . . have grace and favor in them . . . Let nobody blame him; his scorn I approve." Her grief has made her thoughts confused; they go back to her childhood and recall her mother's maid Barbara, who died when her lover deserted her. Barbara's song stays in Desdemona's mind, and she sings it as Emilia helps her to undress. Othello's accusations against her are still rankling; in her innocence she asks Emilia if there really are women who would betray their husband's love. Emilia, practical, unromantic and matter-of-fact, assures her that there are "some such, no question." Desdemona cannot understand it; Emilia, who has no illusions, says that she would do the same if the payment was great enough. She has had no reason to be loyal to her own husband; in her last speech she makes it clear that Iago's treatment of her has been heartless, indifferent, lacking in all consideration for her feelings.

But Desdemona has no desire to return evil for evil; if she has done wrong, she only wishes to learn to do better by suffering.

Commentary

This scene stresses Desdemona's purity and the beauty of her soul. In spite of Othello's cruel treatment, she still loves him. Her submissive obedience to his wishes, her repeated protestations of her love for him, her innocent and unworldly attitude towards men, all serve to heighten the sense of pathos and undeserved suffering which is before her.

As we move into further pathos, Desdemona explains to the audience that her mother had a maid called Barbara who fell in love with a man who went mad. Barbara had a song about a "willow," which is the symbol of a forsaken lover. She died singing that song. When Desdemona has finished explaining this, and Emilia has begun to help her undress, Desdemona begins to sing the same song of her mother's tragic maid. Desdemona's articulation of grief is delivered in the slow cadences of the word "willow" being repeated, and as she sings we share in a profound sense of impending disaster. As her mother's maid Barbara died singing this song, the implication—and there is no attempt at subtlety or ambiguity—is clearly that Desdemona will soon die. It is as if the singing comes as a sad confirmation of what we have been fearing with increasing alarm since Othello slapped Desdemona in the face before Lodovico and the attendants from Venice. The song, deservedly famous in its own right in Elizabethan lyrics, proceeds as follows (and remember that it is sung slowly and with much melancholy):

> The poor soul sat sighing by a sycamore tree,
>> Sing all a green willow;
> Her hand on her bosom, her head on her knee,
>> Sing willow, willow, willow;
> The fresh streams ran by her, and murmur'd her moans;

Sing willow, willow, willow;
Her salt tears fell from her, and soften'd the stones;—
Sing willow, willow, willow.   (lines 41-49)

The song continues a little further, but with broken comments of interrupting dialogue. As Desdemona moves slowly around the room, singing the song slowly and with a faint smile of steadfast love and courage, the audience is moved to pity her and through her to pity all good persons wronged.

Emilia is contrasted in every way with her mistress—she expects very little consideration; still she resents the attitude of the sort of man she knows, Iago. Her reaction to abuse is not Desdemona's submission—her philosophy is "let them know, The ills we do, their ills instruct us so." Desdemona, in spite of what Othello believes, would never commit adultery; but to Emilia, "The world's a huge thing; it is a great price/For a small vice."

Notes

This scene serves several purposes:

1. Desdemona's docility and quiet submission deepen the sense of the coming tragedy.

2. Her questioning of Emilia about the ways of the world serve to emphasize her innocence.

3. Emilia's outbreak against men in her last speech explains a great deal of the background of her life with Iago; it justifies her denunciation of him later on.

4. The contrast between the innocence of Desdemona and the sophistication of her attendant is dramatically effective.

ACT V · SCENE 1

Summary

Roderigo has evidently consented to Iago's urging to kill Cassio, so that Othello and Desdemona will stay on in Cyprus, and give Roderigo an opportunity of continuing with his suit of Desdemona.

Roderigo hides behind the front of a building; Iago stays nearby. He rejoices to himself over the fact that if they are both killed, he will be the gainer. Roderigo is annoying him by requests for the treasure he has given him to hand to Desdemona. Cassio is a true gentleman, and his way of life is a contrast and an irritation to Iago — "He hath a daily beauty in his life That makes me ugly." Moreover, if Cassio lives, he may find out from Othello that Iago has been the one to arrange his attempted murder. They must both die, for Iago's purposes.

As Cassio enters, Roderigo thrusts at him, but Cassio's coat of mail prevents the wound from being fatal. In turn he wounds Roderigo. Iago, unseen, behind Cassio, wounds him in the leg and retires.

Othello enters, hears Cassio's cries for help, but ignores them, except to exult that Iago has kept his word. With ominous threats he goes to seek Desdemona.

Lodovico and Gratiano, the visitors from Venice, enter and hear the cries of Cassio and Roderigo, but are afraid that they may be a trick to lure them to an attack in the dark.

Iago re-enters, as though he had been roused from sleep. Gratiano and Lodovico recognize him by his light. Cassio appeals to Iago for help; Roderigo cries to him also. Hearing his voice, Cassio accuses him of being one of his attackers; Iago seizes the opportunity to stab Roderigo, appearing thus to avenge Cassio.

With Roderigo silenced, Iago begins to cry aloud for more help; he recognizes Lodovico and tells him that the victim of the attack is Cassio. The two Venetians are dismayed. Iago displays great concern for Cassio and binds his wound for him—the wound which he had himself inflicted.

Bianca enters and breaks into grievous cries over Cassio. Iago, always ready to take advantage of any opportunity, throws suspicion upon her. "Gentlemen all, I do suspect this trash To be a party in this injury" — and later "Go know of Cassio where he sup'd tonight . . . What, do you shake at that? . . . Come, mistress, you must tell's another tale."

Iago then calls for a light, and seeing Roderigo, pretends great surprise — "Roderigo! no. Yes, sure O heaven! Roderigo." Hypocritically he asks Cassio what malice there was between them; Cassio, of course, has no idea even of Roderigo's identity. Iago makes sure that Lodovico and Gratiano shall suspect Bianca—"Do you perceive the gastness of her eye? Nay, if you stare, we shall hear more anon. Behold her well; I pray you, look upon her; Do you see, gentlemen? nay, guiltiness will speak, Though tongues were out of use."

Emilia enters to be told the news; she too turns upon Bianca, who protests her innocence. Iago sends her to tell Othello and Desdemona what has happened; this is the crisis of his life—"This is the night That either makes me or fordoes me quite."

Commentary

The development of character takes place in the earlier parts of the play; by now each character is established and has shown growth, improvement or deterioration. Iago's villainy has increased to its greatest extent; Othello's naturally noble nature has been broken and disintegrated by Iago's influence; Desdemona, showing little change, has remained innocent, loving and devoted throughout. Roderigo is not quite the fool he appeared in the first part of the play; before his death he has shown some spirit, and expresses regret as he dies for the part he has played.

Notes

1. This scene brings Iago to the crisis—"This is the night That either makes me or fordoes me quite." If all goes as he hopes, his scheming will come to a successful climax.

2. Suspense is aroused by the doubt as to whether he will succeed or not, for although he manages to do away with Roderigo, Cassio remains alive to menace his safety.

ACT V · SCENE 2

Summary

This scene is the final conclusion or denouement of the play. It takes place in Desdemona's bedchamber, where she lies asleep. Othello enters, fortifying his resolution with the certainty that he has a just cause for putting her to death; it is not jealousy that drives him to it, but the resolve that she must have no more opportunity to do wrong. Her beauty overcomes him; he weeps and kisses her, but without abandoning his purpose.

When she wakes, he gives her an opportunity to pray before she dies. She is afraid of him—"Talk you of killing?. . .And yet I fear you; for you are fatal then When your eyes roll so." Still she is at a loss to know the reason—"Why I should fear I know not, Since guiltiness I know not; but yet I feel I fear." At last Othello accuses her directly of giving his handkerchief to Cassio. She denies it and begs him to bring Cassio to bear out her words. Othello tells her that he has seen Cassio with the handkerchief, and that Cassio has confessed that he loved Desdemona; finally that Cassio is dead. Desdemona's wail of desperation at this news is interpreted by Othello as unbecoming grief for her lover; actually she is dismayed to find that Cassio cannot tell Othello the truth and clear her good name. In spite of her pleading, Othello strangles her. Emilia calls outside the door, while he makes sure that Desdemona dies quickly and painlessly. Distracted by Emilia's knocking, and aghast at the deed he has committed, he draws the curtains around Desdemona's bed and admits Emilia.

Emilia brings news of the murder — Othello of course thinks she refers to Cassio, and is taken aback to hear that it is Roderigo who is slain, while Cassio still lives. "Not Cassio kill'd! then murder's out of tune, And sweet revenge grows harsh." It is appalling to think that Cassio has escaped Desdemona's fate.

They are interrupted by a faint cry from Desdemona, not yet dead. On her death-bed she protests her innocence, and still shields Othello — "A guiltless death I die . . ." and in answer to Emilia's question "Who hath done this deed?" she answers, protecting her husband "Nobody; I myself. Farewell. Commend me to my kind lord. O, farewell!" This lie, uttered to save Othello, only strengthens his belief in her deceit — "She's, like a liar, gone to burning hell, and he confesses his crime —

64

" 'Twas I that kill'd her."

In answer to Emilia's attack upon him, he tells the reason, and quotes Iago as his witness. Emilia is thunderstruck, and can only repeat, in dazed astonishment "My husband!" When she is sure that Othello is in earnest, she protests—"If he say so, may his pernicious soul Rot half a grain a day! he lies to the heart" and breaks into abuse of the Moor—"She was too fond of her filthy bargain." Careless of the consequences, she rails against him and cries aloud for help.

Montano, Gratiano, Iago and others rush in. Emilia loses no time in accusing Iago of false witness. Iago acknowledges that he told Othello that Desdemona had played him false with Cassio, and tries to hush Emilia. But she is not to be subdued by him any longer; she defies him and abuses Othello.

Othello makes no attempt to evade the consequences of his crime; he speaks to her uncle, Gratiano, who tells of her father's death. Othello tells why he killed his wife; to the best of his belief she was unfaithful; Iago is his witness, and he himself saw the fateful handkerchief in Cassio's hand.

Emilia is about to tell all the truth; Iago tries to stab her, but she persists and tells Othello that she found the handkerchief and gave it to Iago, because he had often urged her to steal it. Iago denies her story, but Othello, convinced, runs at Iago, who stabs Emilia and flees. Montano and Gratiano leave, the former to pursue Iago while Gratiano stays by the door to prevent Othello's escape. He is now unarmed.

Emilia, fatally wounded by Iago, lies by her mistress, sings snatches of the willow song, and dies protesting to Othello that Desdemona has always been true to him.

Othello discovers another sword of keen Spanish metal; he asks Gratiano to let him out of the room, or to come in and speak with him, pretending that he is still unarmed.

When Gratiano enters, however, he shows him the weapon, but assures him that he will not use it against him; he has come to the end of his tether, and anyone can defeat him—"Man but a rush against Othello's breast, And he retires." He looks upon Desdemona in a passion of grief and regret, calling down retribution upon his own head.

The rest of the company return with Iago as prisoner, and Cassio, carried in a chair. Othello wounds Iago with his Spanish sword. He asks Cassio's pardon for what he has done, and begs him to ask Iago why he has ruined him. But Iago refuses to speak — "From this time forth I never will speak a word." Othello's only justification is his belief that he was satisfying his honor in murdering Desdemona — "For nought I did in hate, but all in honour."

Lodovico explains the whole matter, by producing a letter found in Roderigo's pocket which tells how Roderigo was to kill Cassio. A second letter, written by Roderigo to Iago, but never sent, was filled with complaints against Iago; evidently Iago had succeeded in winning him over again before it could be sent to him.

Cassio adds to the story by explaining that he had found the handkerchief in his room, where Iago had confessed to dropping it. He goes on to say that Roderigo's letter also told how Iago had persuaded Roderigo to provoke him (Cassio) to the quarrel that led to his dismissal.

Lodovico tells Othello that he must go with them; he is to lose his command, while Cassio becomes governor of Cyprus, and be kept prisoner until the state of Venice decides his fate. Iago is to be treated as he deserves—"if there be any cunning cruelty That can torment him much and hold him long, It shall be his."

Othello asks to be allowed to speak before they go. He recalls his service to the state. He asks them to give an account of his deed which shall be fair, giving all the facts, but making it clear that he did not commit the murder out of malice. He asks them to speak of him as "one that loved not wisely but too well; one not easily jealous, but being wrought perplex'd in the extreme." Then he makes believe to recall an incident in the past, when he punished a Turk for beating a Venetian citizen, and, in illustrating it, he stabs himself with his sword, and falls dead upon the bed. Cassio speaks generously of him, in spite of the wrong that has been done him—"This did I fear, but thought he had no weapon; For he was great of heart."

Lodovico closes the play with a diatribe against Iago; he orders Gratiano to take over the Moor's possessions, as he is his heir, and gives orders for the punishment of Iago, announcing that he must bear the ill news to Venice.

Commentary

The tragedy is brought to its close. Iago has accomplished Othello's downfall, his death and Desdemona's, but he has not succeeded in destroying the Moor's soul. At the end, he becomes again the man we admired at the beginning of the play. Othello has murdered Desdemona as an act of justice and keeps his honor to the end—"An honourable murderer, if you will; For nought I did in hate, but all in honour."

Structure

Methods Of Analyzing Structure

For art to exist in any real way, something has to be *made*. A given work of art, therefore, has some sort of definite structure, even if that structure is an abstract kind of formless entity. The structure of literary works of art is not something uniform. From genre to genre, and within each genre, there are virtually countless kinds of structures. It would be idle work to attempt to discuss the structures of *King Lear* and *The Catcher in the Rye* in the same way. The purpose of this section is to familiarize students with some of the ways in which we can discuss structure, with a particular interest in a Shakespearean drama. After introducing several methods of analyzing structure, we will illustrate the ways in which these methods can be used in answering particular essay questions.

1. Analysis

The first place to start an analysis of structure is in consideration of plot. If plot is, as Aristotle stated, the first principle and soul of tragedy, it seems obvious that we should come to certain conclusions about the plot before passing on to other more sophisticated dimensions. In a certain sense, structure is another word for plot. Both describe what *is*; that is, both direct us to *what happens when*, which is the heart of the drama. The structure, in other words, is the way in which the events of the play are put together. The turning points, reversals, or vicissitudes within the action of the play are all presented in a definite way for a definite purpose. The student's task is to begin by establishing clearly in his mind the *order* of the events and then go on to *explanations* of that order. Most dramatists are, fortunately, logical as well as entertaining. We are not so much called upon to discover their intentions as, rather, the logical reason for things happening when they do. In short, then, the first way in which to begin an analysis of structure is to delineate and explain the plot in all of its changes and reversals.

2. Synthesis

Whereas in "Analysis" we were concerned with presenting the physical division of the work into its parts, as discovered in the plot, now we should make an effort to explain the development of the connections between the parts. What are the elements which link the various stages of the play? If we are considering a tragedy, how does the dramatist allow the play to flow from preparations for the "fall," through the "fall," and finally into the aftermath? Where are the *key* turning points in the plot? How has the dramatist prepared us in the beginning for what will arrive in the ending? In other words, in synthesis, we attempt to draw all of the parts of the play together. It is one thing to divide the work into its parts, and another to explain the ways in which those parts have been logically connected.

More often than not, the student will find that the *motives of the characters* provide the links between the parts. X happens when it does, because Character Y has certain motives. Particularly in tragedy, we discover the importance of characters' motives in explaining the logic of the plot. Obviously, some of the parts of the plot will be joined through contrived "accidents," such as a chance meeting or the discovery of a stolen letter. Since plays are primarily about people, however, more often than not the people in the play become the organizing factors. One character's greed or another one's jealousy will often be sufficient explanation for the fact that everything in the play happens when it does. But whether the student concentrates on character motivation or on the chance events of fortune, he must always be asking whether the structure seems molded in not only a logical but an esthetic way. And this leads us to our next consideration.

3. Esthetic Unity

When the student has divided the work into structural sections, and explained the way in which these sections are held together, he must then decide whether or not the entire framework has esthetic unity. Is the ending artistically derived from the opening? Do the motives of the characters adequately explain their actions? Is there any sort of inconsistency between the characters' motives and actions which the dramatist leaves unexplained? In "Analysis" we divide the action of the play into its logical sections, but now we try to evaluate and to criticize. A good tragedy should have an *introduction*, *rising action*, a *climax*, *falling action*, and a *catastrophe*. That is, we need to be introduced to some of the characters, be told about things which have happened recently before the play's opening, and in general given enough information to understand what happens *in* the play.

In the *rising action* are certain events or revealed attitudes which lead logically into the *climax* or chief turning point in the play. There is usually some sort of *exciting action*, something, some reason which sets the rising action in motion. Sometimes it is the challenge to solve a riddle, other times the desire to avenge a slain relative. But there is always some reason which causes the action to commence. After the climax, certain events lead—and usually quite swiftly—to the final catastrophe, which is usually a multiple death or at least the death of the central character. The structure of most classical and Shakespearian tragedy is in accord with this formula and thus keeping these terms in mind often makes it easier to discuss the structure of *any* play, even if there are modifications which must be made.

Whether or not a tragedy moves skillfully through these stages or their explicit equivalent is the factor upon which our evaluation of the esthetic unity will usually depend. For example, it would not be esthetically satisfying if the death of the hero simply arrived with out any particular climax preceding it. We need to feel the building of certain emotions which are responsible for the catastrophe, and without such a building we feel cheated.

4. Relationship Of Parts To Whole

In all of these approaches, and in countless others which the student will be able to devise for himself, we are concerned in one way or another with the relationship between the parts and the whole. We want to arrive at an understanding of structure by dividing a work, putting it back together, shaking it, and finally coming up with explanations of how it "works." We want to be able to say this play has the following structure and this is why it is or is not successful. Any given scene or act should contribute significantly to the overall structure of a play, for a play is too short for much waste of time. In other words, we address ourselves to the relationship between each of the parts and the whole in order to arrive at an understanding of the whole.

Some critics follow the general approach to the construction of Shakespeare's tragedies outlined and developed by A.C. Bradley in his famous lectures. Bradley explains how a Shakespearian tragedy always depicts some sort of *conflict* between competing forces which ends in *catastrophe*. Every play has three large parts. The first is the *exposition* or early part of the play where the dramatist presents us with certain information, introduces us to the world of the drama and to the characters. The second section is devoted to the complication or conflict —its beginnings, changes, reversals of advantage between the competing forces—and the third shows us the results of the conflict, that is, the catastrophe or conclusion. Often Shakespeare gets the attention of his audience in the opening of a play with a dramatic event—such as the witches in *Macbeth* or the appearance of the ghost of Hamlet's father— and then slows the pace to provide us with certain necessary facts, usually presented through low-keyed conversations with little background action. In short, though, Shakespeare maintains the conflict throughout the play in various ways. There is constant alternation between our fears and our hopes as first one side is up, then another opposing one gathers momentum. The large threefold way of viewing the construction of a Shakespearian play is often very useful, although not all of his plays fit the three-part division easily.

Questions And Answers on Structure

Question 1.

Describe the development of Othello's jealousy as it relates to the structure of the play.

Answer

Othello centers around the rising jealousy which Othello feels as the play progresses. The entire plot turns on the advances and pauses in this cancerous jealousy. In Act II, a chance meeting between Cassio and Desdemona reinforces Iago's idea of developing a suspicion of the two in the mind of Othello. Throughout Act III, Iago fans the fires of Othello's incipient jealousy and the Moor becomes more and more fearful that there really is a romance between his wife and Cassio. When Iago arranges to secure the handkerchief and have Cassio's Bianca seen with it, the play reaches a major turning point. From the moment he sees the handkerchief, Othello is convinced of his wife's guilt. Othello is strengthened even further in his suspicion when (also in Act IV) news is brought—by Lodovico—that Cassio is to replace Othello as commander in Cyprus. Othello's blind jealousy leads him to kill Desdemona, only to discover her innocence too late. In the end, therefore, he kills himself.

The play thus moves as Othello's jealousy dictates.

Iago's motivation for provoking Othello is provided very early in the play when Cassio rather than Iago wins Othello's favor. This may be said to be the *exciting action*. The *rising action* which follows conduces to the strengthening of Othello's doubts and feelings of jealousy. The *climax* arrives when Othello sees the handkerchief which he had given to Desdemona now in the hands of Cassio's mistress Bianca. The *falling action* then follows as Othello rapidly grows more despondent, and events sweep up swiftly to his smothering of Desdemona (at Iago's suggestion) and to his own suicide upon realizing her innocence. The play, in other words, depicts the planting of the seeds of jealousy, the growing of jealous feelings, and the culmination of those feelings in the various murders in the end. There is exposition, conflict, and catastrophe, for the structure is completely dependent upon the jealousy of Othello, which in its growth and horror leads to disaster. The plot explains the logic of the developing jealousy, while the structure of the play demonstrates it.

Question 2.

Is the construction of *Othello* designed to present a sustained alternation of victory between the opposing forces?

Answer

No, for as A.C. Bradley and others have written, *Othello* differs from some of the other plays in this sense. Whereas, in some Shakespeare plays we feel one of the opposing forces advance for a while, and then watch it withdraw as the opposite force gains, in *Othello* there is a clear-cut advance of Iago's evil force all the way up to the end. The first part of the play entertains us and gets us interested in what is happening, but once Iago begins to make Othello feel jealous over Desdemona, we see Othello swept along rapidly to his disaster. There is little alternation, because he gets in, as it were, deeper and deeper. The construction of *Othello* is such, in actuality, that instead of having a sustained alternation of advantage between the opposing forces, we have a rising crescendo of Othello's victimization. In the early parts of the play, Othello is steadfast in his faith in Desdemona's honesty and in Iago's friendship. But once he begins to doubt Desdemona at all, we practically *know* he will find her guilty; it is only a matter of time. As John Donne wrote in a short poem: the first minute after noon is night. Iago's first act is to arouse Desdemona's father to tell him that his daughter has eloped with Othello (he has the foolish, boyish Venetian Roderigo relay this news), and for the rest of the play the extent of his evil potential is steadily enlarged. Even in Act III, when Iago is suggesting Cassio's flirtation with Desdemona, he is far removed from the evil dimensions which surround him by the end of the play.

Question 3.

How does Shakespeare join the various parts of the play?

Answer

Any play is automatically given a physical division into parts through the division made by the five acts, and the scenes within each of those acts. But the connections between those acts are not automatic; rather, Shakespeare must develop a logical sequence of actions which grow naturally out of the characters and the relationships between them. *Othello* moves smoothly and evenly from the early preparations for the tragedy, through a climax, and concludes in disaster. The play has various turning points, each of which serves as a link to what will come. The first turning point, ironically, comes in the very beginning of the play when Iago announces his desire to destroy Othello. Previously, Iago has been Othello's good friend, but now, with the appointment of Cassio to the coveted lieutenant's position, Iago turns away from Othello and plots his downfall. This turning point leads logically and explicitly to other events of Act I, such as Iago's use of Roderigo to inform Brabantio that Othello has eloped with Desdemona. Before we go on to the next turning point, we should notice the extremely delicate way in which Shakespeare establishes certain ideas and phrases which can later be repeated and thus bind the parts of the play together. Thus, for example, in Act I, Scene 3, Brabantio says to Othello: "Look to her, Moor, if thou hast eyes to see:/ She has deceived her father, and may thee" (lines 293-294). Later on, in Act III, Scene 3, line 206, Iago uses the same point to further Othello's jealousy ("She did deceive her father, marrying you," etc.). Thus Shakespeare has carefully introduced an idea early in the play which can be used as a unifying tool later on.

In Act II there is a meeting by mere chance between Cassio and Desdemona which strengthens Iago's preliminary scheme of building a case against them. Then Iago has Roderigo pick a fight with Cassio, who has been drinking. Iago summons Othello who, in annoyance, reduces Cassio's rank. Iago can now suggest to Cassio that he ask Desdemona to intervene with Othello and ask that he be reinstated as lieutenant. Shakespeare has manipulated the plot by having Iago determine the series of events. We see Iago scheming onstage while Shakespeare is determining a skillful plot. The dramatist apparently asked himself, "How can we create a reason for Cassio to need to talk some of the time with Desdemona?" It is evident that to make the Moor jealous it will be necessary for him to see Desdemona and Cassio together. By having Cassio seek Desdemona's help, and by having her act in the interest of Cassio, Shakespeare not only provides for a logical sequence of ideas and actions, but blends in a certain kind of irony which makes Othello's jealousy very unattractive.

Throughout the play, there is this kind of structural development. The chance meeting between Desdemona and Cassio which leads to Iago's scheme which leads to Cassio's punishment which leads to his private talks with Desdemona which leads to Othello's increasing jealousy which leads to his eventual smothering of Desdemona and his own suicide becomes an almost infinite series of connected parts. By having a *logical* sequence of actions, and by explaining those actions in terms of consistency of character action, Shakespeare's structure *becomes* automatic. There is no problem in moving from Iago's revenge motives into the long middle section of the play in which Othello's jealousy grows rapidly, nor is there any difficulty in moving from this section to the final section of multiple murders. The structure of preparation — fall — aftermath becomes more than convenient; it acquires an excitement. We almost can sense in Act I the horrible conclusions which are going to arrive in Act V. The links between the parts of the play, when moving from one section of the play to the next, as well as when moving from one act to the next, all "work" because of their tightly binding *logic*. The characters behave in ways which we consider logical and consistent with their overall patterns of thinking. The scheming Iago, the envious Roderigo, the loyal and good Cassio, the fair Desdemona, and the ignorant Othello all perform their parts in a way which allows the events to grow out of each other into an unbroken logical chain which culminates in death.

Question 4.

What is the relationship between conflict and structure in *Othello?*

Answer

In many Shakespearian tragedies, the conflict begins relatively early in the play. There is a constant alternation of advantage between the opposing forces. The structure of *Othello*, as A.C. Bradley and other Shakespearian critics have noticed, is somewhat different. For, in *Othello*, the central conflict—which is Othello's raging sexual jealousy—is not really worked into the drama until the middle. That is, the construction of the play is such that there is an unusually long exposition and a delayed introduction of the conflict itself. There is a great deal of preparation in Acts I and II, as we have seen, whereby Iago plots the ways in which Othello will first be made aware of a possible relationship between Desdemona and Cassio. But the actual conflict, the real agony, does not begin in *Othello* until the middle of the play, in Act III, gathering great momentum when Othello sees the so-called "proof" of Desdemona's guilt in the handkerchief. Then, once the conflict has been introduced, it grows extremely rapidly and leads almost in a straight line to Desdemona's death in Act V. In other words, instead of having the conflict introduced at an early point in the play, we have the conflict introduced in the middle; and instead of showing an alternation of forces, we only begin late "inside" the force of Othello's wrath and stay with it from then on. The structure of the play is designed somewhat differently, in order to have a mushrooming anger "take over" the entire play. And there is little "relief" between Othello's discovery of guilt and the end of the play, whereas in the first few acts we find occasional scenes or sections of relief, such as some humor, or when men are conferring about the Turks' intended invasion of Cyprus. In the second half of the play, Othello's private, raging passion is center-stage and dominates everything. The rather lengthy preparations for this induced jealousy, undertaken by Iago in the first two acts, thus lead only gradually into something violent and explosive. In a way, the structure of *Othello* bears resemblance to a fuse and a powder keg, where the lighted fuse burns along slowly and evenly in the first few acts and then ignites the powder in the middle of the play. There is not even a suggestion, in the early parts of the play, that Othello is *capable* of such wrath, except for the implicit assumption that he has always been a tough and valorous military man. But even in this dimension of his personality, the times when he just barely escaped from danger are emphasized, not the times when he himself constituted the danger to someone else. Shakespeare has carefully postponed certain characteristics of Othello to a point in the developing structure where those characteristics would have the greatest impact on the audience. The conflict becomes enlarged in its being delayed, and thus the structure of the play is designed to magnify that conflict.

Characters

Character Sketches

Although there is a full discussion of the characters in the answers to the questions and in the chart entitled "Character Delineation", there is also given below a list of the major characters with a brief description of each.

Othello

Othello is a professional soldier and a servant of the state of Venice. He is a Moor, a Moslem Negro from North Africa. Middle-aged, he has fought hard and valiantly all of his life and is being sent to defend Cyprus against an expected attack by the Turks. As a soldier and a man of action, Othello is not particularly inclined to fancy speech, and in fact remarks on the rudeness of his language on several occasions. He is referred to as a "barbarian" by Iago and to a certain extent this is true; he relies on warrior instincts rather than sound reasoning. He is led by Iago to kill his new wife Desdemona and ultimately to his own suicide. We pity him because he is unable to detect the duplicity and evil of Iago. Othello's central flaw is that he believes that all things are what they seem; he has no suspicion that appearances are deceiving, and this leads to his false conviction of Desdemona.

Desdemona

Desdemona is young and very white-skinned, the daughter of Brabantio, a nobleman of Venice. She has gone against the wishes of her father by eloping with Othello. She has fallen in love with Othello primarily because of his great military deeds and his courage. She has not known him very long or very well when they are married secretly. Throughout the play she is innocent and cannot understand what is the "cause" of Othello's jealousy. She is always faithful to him; even when she is dying and asked to name her murderer she does not mention Othello. For the most part Desdemona is passive, acted upon rather than acting. She moves through the play like a pale ghost and we never doubt that she is going to die an unfair death.

Iago

Iago is the villain of the play, the Italian Machiavellian stereotype of the evil man who enjoys doing evil for its own sake. In Shakespeare's source, part of Iago's motivation for ruining Othello and Cassio is his own love for Desdemona but this is not used in Shakespeare's play. Critics have debated Iago's motivation for several centuries and the arguments still continue. Coleridge and others have argued that Iago has a motiveless malignity, while Hazlitt and certain critics have suggested a variety of reasons for Iago's evil, particularly suggesting the love of power as the central motive. In any case, Iago is cunning, crafty, intellectual and intelligent, malicious and demonic, covetous and harmful. He dupes Othello with almost as much ease as he dupes the stupid Roderigo. He enjoys his evil and refuses to explain why he has done the things he has.

Cassio

Cassio is the faithful officer and the servant of Othello. Like Othello he is a professional soldier and his reputation is based on his loyalty to his commanding officer. In the beginning of the play he is appointed to the position of lieutenant to Othello, which indicates that, until later, when he is suspected of having a secret romance with Desdemona, Cassio has earned Othello's highest respect. Cassio has no principal actions in the play; once he is demoted he only tries to enlist the aid of Desdemona. This leads to Othello's increasing suspicion that Cassio and Desdemona are secret lovers. In the end of the play, Cassio is in command in Cyprus and thus is the most unchanged character in the play; he begins and ends as a dutiful soldier and servant of the state of Venice.

Roderigo

Roderigo is a fool and a ridiculous example of a soldier. He is in the play as something of a Frankenstein monster in the service of his master Iago. He does whatever Iago tells him to do, always in the hope of winning the love of Desdemona. It never seems to occur to him that his chances for ever marrying Desdemona are virtually nonexistent. He gives money and jewelry to Iago to give to Desdemona but Iago keeps everything for himself. At the end of the play Roderigo is killed by

Cassio and Iago after he has tried to ambush Cassio on Iago's instructions. He never achieves any happiness in the play and only serves in a technical manner, assisting the execution of Iago's malicious plans.

Emilia

Emilia is the woman of the world, the woman experienced in all aspects of life but particularly in sexual escapades. She is a fairly coarse and almost hard-boiled woman, and at the same time she is the gentle and loving servant to Desdemona whom she loves very much. Her one wrong action—giving the handkerchief to Iago—is performed in ignorance and done from the simple motive of the desire to please her husband. She has sufficient respect for what is right and just, and sufficient love for Desdemona, that she willingly denounces Iago and explains his evil role in the strange course of misunderstood events. She would rather lose Iago as a husband than tolerate his blatant and offensive villainy. Because of her experience and realism she provides a sharp contrast to Desdemona's innocence and idealism.

Methods of Analyzing Characters

Describing the Characters

It is always a good idea to begin any commentary on characters with a brief description of each of them—what they are like, what they seem to think about themselves, etc. This kind of brief survey of the characters assures the student that he will not assume too much when discussing the characters in more complex or sophisticated ways. It also forces the student not to overlook any of the various characters' essential attributes. It should be pointed out that Hamlet is the young prince of Denmark, or that Othello is a Moor; then these simple facts should be amplified by whatever else we know. For example, in Shakespeare's source, a Moor was only a man converted to Islam on the northern coast of Africa, but in the play, Shakespeare has quite explicitly made his Moor a Negro, carefully presenting multiple references to Othello's blackness in the very opening act of the play — particularly in the remarks of the outraged Brabantio. Also, if Shakespeare does not tell us a great deal about a particular character, this should be pointed out. If we do not learn enough about Emilia it is perhaps because Shakespeare does not want to detract too much attention from Desdemona. All in all, then, one should make a short survey of the characteristics — both emotional and physical — of the characters.

Analysis of Character Development

Probably the most important aspect of character analysis is the treatment of the development of the characters, and primarily the main characters. It is all-important to explain how a character *changes* in the course of the play. And one must also explain *why* those changes take place *when* they do. Even if a character seems static throughout, there must be an explanation. It may be that Shakespeare is using the character as a prop, a necessary convenience, or simply as an illustrative example of an alternative to the mode of existence courted by the hero or heroine. When certain emotions—such as greed, hate, love, revenge, bitterness, confidence—come to the surface, we should try to understand precisely how and why. Is there violent reaction or calm acceptance? Does Lady Macbeth's incipient guilt plunge her into a quasi-psychotic depression? The basic changes, not the minor ones, should be briefly delineated and more thoroughly analyzed. Is it right that a certain character feels as he does? Is it human or is it extreme? Abnormal or normal? Unusual or typical? Surprising or expected? Are changes foreshadowed? Are they ever illogical or too contrived? All literary analysis consists of an extended process of asking questions. And this questioning process is particularly vital to the analysis of characters. We must understand why characters behave and change in order to understand the meaning of the entire play. Aside from all the usual reasons that characters change, as, for example, when one's mother or relative is killed and one suddenly is filled with a desire for revenge and acts accordingly, many explanations of character change can be found either in their motivation, as it is developed by the dramatist, or by the demands of the themes. And these will be our next two considerations.

Motivation

In considering the motivation of characters we are fundamentally enlarging our answer to the "why" of character behavior. Shakespeare is of course very "modern" in his grasp of human psychology and the ways in which thought should be translated into action. We recall that the original exciting action in *Othello* is Iago's motivation of revenge. But revenge can not become a catch-all expression for summarizing everything that Iago does. He is not simply a human being who feels wronged (through the appointment of the Florentine, bookish Cassio to a position which Iago had worked for), but, first and finally, a *human being*. That is to say, Iago has certain mixed emotions which contribute unequally to his desire to harm Othello. He may have a deep sexual jealousy of Othello, for example, and resent the apparent ease with which Othello has gained Desdemona. Othello himself, on the other hand, may become quickly over-angry at Desdemona because of a deep insecurity over class. That is, although of royal lineage, Othello is nevertheless beneath the upper level of Venetian society into which he has made a precipitous marriage. His desire to be equal, socially, is evident in his very first lines of the play when he tells Iago that he is, after all, worthy of Desdemona. In other words, in discussing motivation, we are trying to describe, as extensively as possible, the total psychological make-up of a character. Then we discover and interpret his uniqueness through the actions brought about by his psychology. Sometimes there is an absence of motivation; at least there *appears* to be such an absence (and let us not, like Othello, think that things are what they seem). Poor Desdemona can not hate Othello even after he has unjustly accused her, because she simply does not understand his jealousy. She has no particular motivation toward revenge. And, as we will mention shortly, Iago often behaves in an unmotivated way in order to fulfill the demands being placed upon him as a thematic character (see next section). In any case, no survey of a play's characters would be complete without explanations of behavior.

Thematic Characters

Often we discover that the behavior of certain characters can be explained by themes. That is, a character like Iago may act in evil ways consistently because allegorically he represents evil. The play is about the destruction wrought by evil and thus Iago may be said to be a "thematic character," less human and less complicated, while more conventional and "stock." Any character in any play may be thought of as a thematic character from one point of view or another, but we generally limit our use of the term to characters who clearly represent certain dominant abstractions which are clashing in a play—i.e., good and evil, love and hatred, loyalty and disloyalty, faithfulness and unfaithfulness (notice how all are extensions of good and evil). Most tragedies involve thematic characters, but not in such ways that we choose to discuss the characters in those terms. In general, it is better to search for what is human or unique about certain characters, but it is always worthwhile to mention briefly the thematic possibilities of the characters. Why are they in the play? Why do they behave as they do? How does their behavior demonstrate particular ideas?

Analyzing Character Relationships

Although inherent in the other methods, the analysis of the relationships between the characters can be used as complete analysis in itself. The world of the play, as we suggested earlier, is largely defined by the nature of the different relationships. Iago has very specific and unusual relationships with both Othello and Roderigo, for example, and the two relationships show us different things about Iago, on the one hand, and confirm some of the same things on the other. In a way, both Roderigo and Othello are Iago's dupes or pawns. But the equation between Othello and Roderigo does not hold when we compare their respective emotions of courage, love, and fear. Emilia is more than a maid to Desdemona and something less than a wife to Iago. Bianca is not simply a whore to Cassio, and Cassio is more than a good lieutenant to Othello. The "more" or the "less" of the basic relationships of friendship, marriage, command, etc., must be clarified, for through this clarification of relationships, we arrive at a greater understanding of the characters themselves.

Character Delineation Chart

	OTHELLO	DESDEMONA	IAGO	CASSIO	RODERIGO	EMILIA
1. Character "type"	professional soldier	innocent	villain	faithful officer	fool	"experienced" woman and wife
2. Central Motivation	love of Desdemona	love of Othello	ruin of Cassio and Othello	loyalty to Othello	love of Desdemona	love of Iago
3. Principal action(s)	kills Desdemona, kills himself	none	works for downfall of Cassio and Othello	none	stabs Cassio	gives handkerchief to Iago; exposes Iago as villain.
4. Principal emotion(s) and attribute	love and jealousy — pride	love — innocence	hate — villainy	loyalty — professionalism	love — childish stupidity	loyalty — misguided faith
5. At the beginning of the play	happy new husband, servant of the State of of Venice	happy new bride	jealous "ancient"	promoted to position of Othello's lieutenant	jealous fool	not seen
6. At the end of the play.	jealous husband, dead by suicide.	wrongfully murdered.	sentenced to death by torture	in command of Cyprus	stabbed by Iago	stabbed by Iago

Questions and Answers on the Characters

Question 5.

Discuss the *development* of Othello as a character. Does he ever become "complicated"? Does he begin and end by thinking in iron-clad "absolutes"?

Answer

Othello changes but does not develop, at least not until the very end of the play, when he feels profoundly repentent over his unjustified deed and displays a sincere and tender love for his murdered wife. This is the sensitive and loving Othello whose positive side has been hidden most of the time. Let us, for a moment, consider Othello as we meet him in the opening of the play. He is a Moor, and one that Shakespeare has deliberately made a Negro as well; he is a renowned military leader, a great soldier, and one of the strong defending arms in the service of the state; he is a man who, through military training, perhaps, has learned to think in absolutes and to make quick decisions; his survival has often depended on quick action rather than on lengthy or studied considerations; he is a lonely man in the sense that he is a black Moor among the Venetian senators; he has been the guest of Brabantio and white society and, although proud of his heritage, realizes that he is to a certain extent alone. Desdemona has fallen in love with him primarily because of his valorous deeds and for the dangers he has survived; as Othello explains to his accusers in Act I, Scene 3:

> My story being done,
> She gave me for my pains a world of sighs:
> She swore, in faith, 'twas strange, 'twas passing strange,
> 'Twas pitiful, 'twas wondrous pitiful: . . .
> She loved me for the dangers I had pass'd,
> And I loved her that she did pity them.
> This only is the witchcraft I have used.   (lines 158-169)

Said otherwise: Othello appealed to Desdemona's imagination and to her inherent attraction to physical courage. This is our central picture of Othello: the successful warrior, more a man of action than an intellectual, more a doer than a thinker.

This picture of the soldier is strengthened when we first see Othello placed in new command of Cyprus; then in his joyful announcement that the Turks have been in a storm and will not attack. When Iago begins to make Othello jealous in the all-important third scene of the third act, we sense Othello's rapid suffering; Othello knows himself well enough that once he decides Desdemona is unfaithful, then he will hold firm to that decision; at the same time, however, he will not make such a decision on little evidence:

> Think'st thou I'd made a life of jealousy,
> To follow still the changes of the moon

With fresh suspicions? No; to be once in doubt
Is once to be resolved.   (lines 177-180)

In other words, once he does have a real doubt, he will work to resolve that doubt immediately—no matter what this entails or what consequences may ensue.

When Othello has slapped Desdemona in the face and called her a whore, before Lodovico and the party from Venice with the announcement of Cassio's new command, Lodovico asks:

Is this the noble Moor whom our full senate
Call all in all sufficient? Is this the nature
Whom passion could not shake? Whose solid virtue
The shot of accident, nor dart of chance,
Could neither graze nor pierce?   (Act IV, Sc. 1, lines 275-279)

Iago immediately issues an understatement, simply saying that Othello has "changed." The point is that certain latent human emotions in Othello have been brought to the surface; Othello may have "changed" as Iago suggests, but he has not "developed" in the sense of having become any more complex. He is still basically a simple character, and striking out at Desdemona is example enough that he still thinks in terms of rash physical violence and retribution.

Othello's jealousy does make him increasingly vulnerable. When he has the proof of the handkerchief, he knows that Desdemona is unfaithful, and once he knows this he also knows that he will punish her—swiftly and physically. As the play moves toward Desdemona's murder, Othello is not developing, but rather becoming increasingly jealous and increasingly hateful. He moves like a frustrated animal and a weary soldier all the way to the very end, when he is at last broken down and moved by remorse and tenderness. He has operated on a "brute," rather than a complicated, level throughout the play.

Question 6.

To what extent may Iago be said to be a thematic character, embodying evil for evil's sake?

Answer

A valid argument can be made that Iago is purely a thematic character, the personification of the force of evil, which leads to the destruction of Othello and Desdemona. Many critics have demonstrated the futility of explaining Iago's hatred of Othello. In the source of the play, Cinthio's novel, Iago is somewhat in love with Desdemona and this becomes a major motive for working for the downfall of Desdemona's husband. But Shakespeare has quite deliberately changed this story; Iago's love for Desdemona is mentioned only once, in his soliloquy at the end of Act II, Scene 1:

The Moor, howbeit that I endure him not,
Is of a constant, loving, noble nature:

> And I dare think he'll prove to Desdemona
> A most dear husband. Now, I do love her too;
> Not out of absolute lust, though peradventure
> I stand accountant for as great a sin . . .   (lines 297-302)

Shakespeare makes no further reference to any love which Iago may bear toward Desdemona, although in the erotic lie wherein Iago describes Cassio's dreaming of Desdemona to Othello, we see the evidence of what is perhaps a confined, repressed lust.

For the most part, then, Iago has very little motivation for his evil behavior; the external fact of Cassio's appointment receives very little discussion after the opening of the play. And when Iago steps forward in soliloquies and describes, gleefully, his forthcoming evil acts, we begin to suspect that he does indeed have what Coleridge termed a "motiveless malignancy." Continually we see the image of Iago as an evil spider ensnaring the innocent and helpless fly: for example, in Act II, Scene 1, upon seeing Desdemona touch Cassio's palm, Iago brags, "With as little a web as this will I ensnare as great a fly as Cassio" (lines 169-170). Or again, in the next major scene, referring to his plan of having Desdemona argue in behalf of Cassio to Othello, Iago confides:

> So will I turn her virtue into pitch,
> And out of her own goodness make the net
> That shall enmesh them all.   (lines 366-368)

Iago *enjoys* his evil acts too much for them to require motives; everything he does or says works directly toward the central conflict of the play.

Like Othello, Iago is not a developing character for he remains loyal to his ideal—or anti-ideal if you will—of malicious revenge. He is confident from the start in his ability to make Desdemona look guilty, even though he does not know how. After Emilia has found the handkerchief, she reflects that Iago has often asked her to secure it; in other words, Iago has been thinking of such a ploy all along. The use of the handkerchief is not a complete accident: it is, we suspect, one of several possibilities imagined by Iago. Iago is a scheming, yet fascinating, character and to say that he is *only* a thematic character seems to divest him of certain human characteristics such as the extreme enjoyment of his evil acts, his logical development of a foundation to support Othello's aroused jealous suspicions, and his conversation with Emilia. After all, most pure-devil characters are not even married. Shakespeare has chosen to give Iago a wife—one who is frankly realistic, as is seen in her discussion of unfaithfulness with Desdemona. Although we notice then that Iago is placed in a human position—that of husband, soldier, etc.—we still must conclude that he is *primarily* a character who creates evil for the sake of creating evil. When Emilia discovers that Iago is behind Othello's false doubts and thus the murder of Desdemona, she underlines Iago's essential "villainy":

> Villainy, villainy, villainy!
> I think upon't, I think: I smell't: O villainy!—
> I thought so then, I'll kill myself for grief:—
> O villainy, villainy! (Act V, Sc. 2, lines 190-193)

These references are more than enough to remind us of what we have known all along: Iago is in the play with the explicit purpose of being the villain; evil is his *raison d'etre*. Evil is his very nature and thus Boas has rightly termed him "the arch-criminal of Shakespearean drama."

Question 7.

Briefly contrast Desdemona and Emilia.

Answer

With the exception of Bianca, Cassio's mistress, who has very little to say, Desdemona and Emilia are the only two women in the play. In Desdemona and Emilia, Shakespeare has presented a striking contrast between innocence and experience, or between idealism and realism. For Desdemona is a sweet unsuspecting creature; even as she slowly seems to realize that Othello plans to kill her, she acts normally. When he enters her bedchamber to murder her, she simply and calmly asks him to come to bed—even though she has had her wedding sheets placed on the bed, hinted to Emilia that she fears some disaster ahead, and sung a song which her mother's maid sang on the eve of her own death. Desdemona, in other words, is faithful to her own love. She fell in love with Othello for what many of us would consider the wrong reasons, but nevertheless she is constant in that love. Even when Othello has mercilessly slapped her, she refuses to lose her composure.

Emilia, on the other hand, as the wife of Iago, is expectedly hardened. She is a woman of the world, a Wife of Bath type, who makes no pretense at innocence and even suggests openly that she would allow her appetites to lead into adultery. Emilia is able to serve Desdemona in a loyal way; in fact, she loves Desdemona very much, as is seen clearly in the last act of the play. Like any woman she wants her husband's approval — which is why she is willing to give Iago the handkerchief — and in this one emotion she has something in common with Desdemona. Emilia is coarse and aware of her sex; however, she remains relatively quiet until the last act when she openly damns Othello for killing Desdemona and fearlessly calls the alarm. While Emilia has no understanding of Desdemona's blind faithfulness and innocence, she is able to proclaim and defend it before Othello at the end of the play. Her own husband is not satisfactory, and yet she is relatively loyal to him until she discovers his major harmful act.

All things considered, the contrast between Desdemona and Emilia is designed primarily to heighten our awareness of Desdemona's innocence and incredible loyalty to Othello. Emilia is in the play—as is

Bianca—to show us that most women are, after all, coarse, fickle, lusty, and bothersome. Desdemona is the exception, of course, and in the contrast she acquires even greater illumination, becoming the bright moral light of the play. At the same time, however, Emilia is no harlot like Bianca, and she bravely goes against her husband in order to see justice done at the end of the play.

Question 8.

Discuss Othello's estimation of Iago. Why is Othello duped so easily?

Answer

Iago has been a professional soldier for a considerable length of time and he is understandably annoyed when he sees Othello choose Cassio as his lieutenant. Why Othello chose Cassio instead of Iago is unknown and in some ways surprising, for Cassio does not have the finesse of Iago. Othello's central view of his "ancient," (that is, his underofficer) is that he is *honest*. In the opening of Act II, Scene 3, Othello tells Cassio to look after the men that night and keep peace; Cassio notes that Iago has been given directions, and Othello replies, "Iago is most honest." A little later, after the outbreak of violence, Othello demands of Iago what has happened. Iago pretends that he does not want to incriminate Cassio, but in so doing makes Cassio look extremely guilty. In other words, Othello is easily fooled—even controlled—by Iago. Othello replies:

> I know, Iago,
> Thy honesty and love doth mince this matter,
> Making it light to Cassio. Cassio, I love thee;
> But never more be officer of mine.   (lines 246-249)

Again Othello refers to Iago's honesty. Iago, on the other hand, lies frequently that he loves Othello very much; for example, when noting that Cassio has just left Desdemona (in Act III, Sc. 3), Iago again pretends that he hates to tell Othello anything which might make him unhappy, but he maintains that he loves Othello too much to maintain silence: "I humbly do beseech you of your pardon/ For too much loving you." Othello's reply is, "I am bound to thee for ever," a statement which suggests the spider-fly relationship between Iago and Othello.

The entire relationship between Iago and Othello is basically static: Othello incorrectly thinks Iago is "honest," while Iago deliberately lies and deceives Othello at every turn. The reason for this is that Othello himself is honest and thus unable to think ill of Iago. It simply never occurs to him that someone who appears as honest as Iago could do him any harm. This is the same emotion experienced by Desdemona in her relationship to Othello and the parallel is an ironic one. Only when Iago has strongly suggested that Desdemona and Cassio are secret lovers does Othello's manner of addressing Iago change: "Villain, be sure thou prove my love a whore,/ Be sure of it; give me the ocular proof" (Act III, Sc. 3, lines 359-360).

Othello is easily duped by Iago because Othello believes in appearances. This, as we shall discuss later on, is one of the main points of the play: things are not always what they seem. Unfortunately, Iago understands Othello's central weakness, for he states clearly at the end of the first act:

> The Moor is of a free and open nature,
> That thinks men honest that but seem to be so,
> And will as tenderly be led by the nose
> As asses are. (lines 405-408)

Iago knows not only that Othello is deceived easily by appearances, but also that Othello is convinced of Iago's honesty. This knowledge defines and determines the relationship between them. There is such a short amount of time between Othello's discovery of Iago's evil duplicity and the end of the play that it is senseless to discuss Othello's change or a change in the nature of the relationship.

Question 9.

Briefly describe Roderigo's motivation and his role within the play.

Answer

Roderigo is boyish, foolish and even at times unusually stupid, yet we never feel ourselves condemning him. This is explained partly by Roderigo's motivation: he is very much in love with Desdemona and has been for some time. He is willing to do anything in order to attain her and that she is so very unattainable makes him that much more pathetic. He hands himself over to Iago in the very beginning of the play for he knows that he himself has not the genius nor the scheming to win Desdemona; in other words, Roderigo at least has a certain amount of self-knowledge and an awareness of his fundamental limitations—which from one point of view puts him above some of the other characters in the play. In any case, Roderigo's honest and recognized love for Desdemona makes him at least acceptable in our eyes, and we feel very sorry for him when he is so cruelly killed by Iago.

Roderigo is in *Othello* for several reasons. In the first place, it is necessary that the villain of the play have some sort of helper or agent to assist in the execution of heinous, secretive acts; Iago quite explicitly has Roderigo come to Cyprus disguised for this very reason. In the second place, Roderigo is a man who goes to great trouble because of his love for Desdemona, and in this sense he shares a motivational logic with the jealous Othello. And finally, Iago's total mastery and manipulation of Roderigo show us how Iago will also be able to master and manipulate the confused Othello. The three objects of Iago's evil deeds—Othello, Cassio, *and* Roderigo—serve to underline the inadequacy of *all* of them to resist the scheming Iago. There is a basic difference, however, in that Roderigo alone knows all along that Iago is scheming; Othello and Cassio are completely unsuspecting. In any case, Roderigo's presence in the play is vital to the development of the plot, while at the same time allowing Shakespeare to present us with another of his justly famous ignorant lovers.

Question 10.

Explain Othello's jealousy and his motivation for killing Desdemona.

Answer

It is easy enough to say that Othello murders Desdemona because he becomes excessively jealous, believing a relationship between her and Cassio. But there is more than sexual jealousy involved. True, the "beast" in Othello is aroused by Iago's suggestions and his erotic relation of Cassio's supposed dream about Desdemona, but is the "beast" really Othello? In a certain sense Othello undergoes an atavistic transformation which turns him back toward the ways of his more primitive ancestry. Othello is a savage who has been tamed through his association with the lords and senators of the republic of Venice; the effect of Iago's schemes is to untame him, as it were, and release him into a world where acts can be justified by the laws of the jungle. If this sounds too much like a way of simplifying Othello, it is nevertheless easily demonstrated as fact in the course of the play, and particularly in Act III, Scene 3, where Othello for the first time almost savagely warns Iago that he had better be telling the truth. It is the beast in Othello that slaps Desdemona before Lodovico and the party from Venice; however, in the final moments of rage, Othello is transformed back into a man who is gentle and tender. We see him in his preparation to kill Desdemona as a man disturbed, not an animal aroused. Phrased differently, Othello is reduced to a more animalistic plane when in the process of becoming more and more jealous, but our final view of him is that of the desperate and unhappy husband; animals, we might note, do not marry.

Jealousy alone, furthermore, is not the sole explanation of Othello's motivation for killing Desdemona. Certainly Othello's honor is involved. We have seen several instances in the play where "reputation" has been given notice and importance. The first main statement arrives when Othello demotes Cassio from his office as lieutenant; Cassio's immediate reaction is:

> Reputation, reputation, reputation! O, I have lost my reputation! I have lost the immortal part of myself, and what remains is bestial. My reputation, Iago, my reputation!
> (Act II, Sc. 3, lines 262-265).

There is a fear that the loss of reputation leaves man a mere

85

beast—and Othello does not want this to happen to him either.

In Act III, Scene 4, Emilia asks Desdemona about Othello, "Is he not jealous?" Desdemona's reply is, "Who, he? I think the sun where he was born/Drew all such humours from him" (lines 29-31). Desdemona never thinks Othello is jealous, for she has only seen the attractive, courageous emotions displayed in his behavior. The simple truth is that she does not know Othello very well and did not know him very well when they were married. Emilia asks, "Is not this man jealous?" and Desdemona replies, "I ne'er saw this before./Sure there's some wonder in this handkerchief:/I am most unhappy in the loss of it" (lines 99-102). Desdemona has never witnessed any jealousy in Othello and thus naively believes that the magical handkerchief is responsible for the change in his behavior. Still in the same scene (Act III, Sc. 4), Emilia explains the nature of jealousy to the innocent Desdemona:

> But jealous souls will not be answer'd so;
> They are not ever jealous for the cause,
> But jealous for they are jealous: 'tis a monster
> Begot upon itself, born on itself. (lines 159-162)

Desdemona's immediate comment is simply, "Heaven keep that monster from Othello's mind!" She does not realize her wish is being made too late. While Othello's jealousy has been aroused—and Shakespeare implies it was always there potentially—he nevertheless kills Desdemona out of pride, anger, and honor. To make Othello only one more jealous husband is a grave oversimplification of character and an underestimation of Moorish temperament.

Meaning

Methods of Analyzing Meaning

Sometimes, it is noted, we forget about the forest because we are too busy looking at the individual trees. In this sense we are apt to avoid commenting on the fundamental meaning of a work of art because we are so concerned with character, structure, and style. Although it is obvious that we cannot avoid completely the implications of the various components of a play as they bear on its meaning, the fact remains that we should take the time to make some sort of general statement about what Shakespeare is trying to tell us. And once we have decided on the meaning, we then can attempt to evaluate the play, to measure it against other plays which treat the same ideas.

1. Explaining the Theme

The student's first task is to denote and explain the central theme of the play. This is not always easily done and, in fact, one sometimes must conclude that there are several themes combined throughout the play. Sometimes—but not often—there is no theme at all. The theme is the central and major idea of the work; in drama the theme is usually an abstract idea or argument which becomes real and concrete through the actions of the characters; as critics we must translate action back into thought, just as the playwright first translated thought into action.

2. Conventions

Usually the dramatist transports us into the world of the play through various dramatic conventions. We must ask how we, the audience, are transported into the minds of the characters. We must try to determine how we are made to believe certain ideas—how, in other words, does the dramatist convince us of the meaning of something? If we are led to believe that love is evil, how does the dramatist lead us to this belief? Meaning is not something easily determined and its presentation must often be clearly understood in order for us to determine precisely *why* such-and-such appears to be true.

3. Unusual or Conventional

The student must answer a basic question when discussing meaning: is it a conventional idea or an unusual one? For example, if the theme of the play is that revenge often only leads to further misery, we can speak of the theme as being "conventional." That is, the idea of the play is one which has been presented many times; it is an *established theme*. On the other hand, a play's main point might be very unusual. If a play's argument is that people who live in glass houses *should* throw stones, the play is making an unusual or uncommon point. Almost every play can be described, in its meaning, as being either conventional or unconventional; and once this is done, the student must explain the ways in which it is or is not conventional.

4. Relating Plot to Meaning

Probably the best way to begin one's analysis of the meaning of a play is to trace very briefly the main plot development in the play. In other words, we need to make a short synopsis of the action before we can make a general statement about the meaning. Then, as we become more particular in our comments on the meaning, we should introduce more particular use of the plot. In other words, we are concerned with making the *level* of our analysis correspond to the level of our explication of the plot. The broad statement needs a broad grasp of the plot, while the "fine points" need more particular textual backing.

5. Logic

As a final check on our understanding of the play we should make some attempt to ascertain whether or not the meaning is logically developed. If the theme somehow seems contradicted by the behavior of one or more characters, or if the relationship between two of the characters argues against the main idea of the play, then we have a problem of logic — which can mean either that the dramatist has not

Meaning Chart:
Othello's Jealousy in Relation to Character & Structure

	DESDEMONA	IAGO	CASSIO	RODERIGO	EMILIA
ACT I	Completely in love with Othello; obviously no "cause" for jealousy.	Decides to make Othello miserable — this leads to Othello's jealousy	His promotion enrages Iago, prompting Iago to scheme against Othello.	Persuaded to aid Iago.	
ACT II		Makes Cassio drunk; after Cassio is then demoted, Iago can persuade him to ask the help of Desdemona—which will later make Othello jealous.	After demotion, persuaded by Iago to seek help from Desdemona.	Fights with Cassio as instructed by Iago; fight leads to Cassio's demotion, which leads to Cassio's relationship with Desdemona	
ACT III	Asks Othello to be kind to poor Cassio thus making Othello increasingly jealous.	Makes it appear, in countless ways, that Cassio and Desdemona are having secret romance.	Seen by Othello when sneaking away guiltily from Desdemona.		Gives Iago the handkerchief which he will use in scheme to make Othello jealous.
ACT IV	Cannot produce handkerchief when asked for it by Othello, thus making him very jealous. Later is struck by Othello when Cassio is put in Cyprus command	Suggests the jealous Othello strangle Desdemona.	Is heard in lewd conversation on Bianca by Othello who thinks that Desdemona is the woman to whom he refers.	Persuaded by Iago to waylay Cassio.	Testifies to Desdemona's innocence but fails to convince the very jealous Othello
ACT V	Swears she is innocent, but is nevertheless smothered by Othello at the peak of his jealousy.	Is discovered to have made Othello falsely jealous.		Wounds Cassio	Reveals Iago's deceit with handkerchief, thus showing Othello his jealousy has been unfounded, which makes Othello kill himself.

done an expert job, or that we have misunderstood the meaning of the play. If our "interpretation" of a play is correct, we should be able to demonstrate logically why it is correct, while, on the other hand, if our interpretation is incorrect, a final check of the logic will force us into reconsideration and probably a revised, improved understanding of the play.

Questions and Answers on Meaning

Question 11.

Describe the basic meaning of *Othello*.

Answer

In *Othello* Shakespeare shows us the malignant effects of a base human emotion, jealousy. This general statement can be supported by a brief survey of what happens in the play. Iago, an Italian filled with wickedness — that is, a conventional villain of Elizabethan drama — convinces the warrior Othello that his wife Desdemona is being unfaithful by having a secret romance with Othello's lieutenant Michael Cassio. Brought to a state of jealousy and uncontrollable suspicions, Othello vows to protect his honor by punishing Desdemona. In the end of the play Othello smothers Desdemona in her bed and then learns that Iago has tricked him, has deceived him into believing that Desdemona had been unfaithful when in fact she had been loyal. Upon discovering Desdemona's innocence too late, Othello is overwhelmed by guilt and commits suicide. Thus, false jealousy has resulted in the deaths of both Othello and his wife.

In the principal scene of the play, Act III, Scene 3, when Iago is first planting the seeds of jealousy in Othello, he makes a central statement about the nature of jealousy:

> O, beware, my lord, of jealousy;
> It is the green-eyed monster which doth mock
> The meat it feeds on: that cuckold lives in bliss
> Who, certain of his fate, loves not his wronger;
> But, O, damned minutes tells he o'er
> Who dotes, yet doubts, suspects, yet strongly loves!

(lines 165-170)

This is perhaps *the* central statement of the play's meaning. The idea is that jealousy has a uniquely horrible self-contained dilemma: one hates and loves at the same time. For Othello is very much in love with Desdemona while at the same time he hates her for being unfaithful. The combination of love and hatred proves too much for any one individual for it thrusts him into a world of contradictions; notice the agony of vacillation in Othello's following lines:

> I think my wife be honest and think she is not;
> I think that thou art just and think thou art not.

I'll have some proof. Her name, that was as fresh
As Dian's visage, is now begrimed, and black
As mine own face. (lines 384-388)

Shakespeare presents several times and in different ways the strange mixture of love and hate which Othello comes to feel toward Desdemona; at no place in the play is the mixture seen more clearly—and even beautifully—than in the opening scene of Act IV where Othello tries to bring himself to a statement damning her while at the same time reminding himself of all her good attributes. Othello struggles to condemn her while at the same time he experiences the extent of his great love for her purity and gentleness. The conversation with Iago, in part, proceeds this way:

Othello: A fine woman! a fair woman! a sweet woman!

Iago: Nay, you must forget that.

Othello: Ay, let her rot, and perish, and be damned tonight; for she shall not live: no, my heart is turned to stone; I strike it, and it hurts my hand. O, the world hath not a sweeter creature: she might lie by an emperor's side and command him tasks.

Iago: Nay, that's not your way.

Othello: Hang her! I do but say what she is: so delicate with her needle: an admirable musician: O! she will sing the savageness out of a bear: of so high and plenteous wit and invention—

Iago: She's the worse for all this.

Othello: O, a thousand thousand times: and then, of so gentle a condition! (lines 188-204)

The mixture of love and hate is clearly seen and we both pity and loathe Othello. And little by little we see the disastrous effects of jealousy growing out of this love-hate formula; even when Othello is murdering Desdemona, he is filled with love and tenderness. But the point of the play is that jealousy cannot be stopped once it is started, and once it is started it can only lead to ruin. Early in the play Iago announces his scheme to place Othello "into a jealousy so strong/ That judgement cannot cure" (Act II, Sc. 1, lines 310-311). The action of the play bears out Iago's prophecy with alacrity and determination.

Question 12.

How does the theme of jealousy connect to the human power of reasoning? Is this connection logical?

Answer

At the same time as jealousy and its ill effects are being demonstrated, the audience is given a certain amount of information about the uses of human reason. As R.B. Heilman and others have shown, there is a dichotomy between witchcraft and wit throughout the play. By this is meant that the powers of reasoning are pitted against the more "magical" powers of love. Immediately prior to his suicide, Othello explains that all will have to refer to him as "one that loved not wisely but too well" (Act V, Sc. 2, line 344). This is the conclusion to a battle of wisdom or "wit" against ignorance which has been continuing throughout the play.

Near the very end of the first act, Iago explains to Roderigo that Othello and Desdemona will be undone by his "wit"; as he states it, it becomes a challenge to him and the forces of evil:

> If sanctimony and a frail vow betwixt an erring barbarian and
> a supersubtle Venetian be not too hard for my wits and all the
> tribe of hell, thou shalt enjoy her."

Iago uses his wit, his scheming or cunning, to make it appear that Desdemona is having a secret romance with Cassio. Furthermore, Iago knows that part of his victory will be determined by the extent to which he can successfully lead Othello into "madness." That is, Iago, using human reasoning, wants to undo his opposition by breaking down its power of reasoning. When Iago speaks of driving Othello into a jealousy so profound that even judgment will not work, he further hopes to drive Othello "even to madness" (Act II, Sc. 1, 320). When Iago instructs Othello to spy on him talking with Cassio, Iago notes that when Cassio smiles, Othello "shall go mad; and his unbookish jealousy must construe/ Poor Cassio's smiles, gestures and light behaviour/ Quite in the wrong" (Act IV, Sc. 1, 101-104). The "unbookish" jealousy means that jealousy is unlearned, that jealousy is the logical relative of ignorance, just as cunning necessarily requires intelligence. The logical connections cannot be questioned, for throughout the play Iago is pictured as intelligent and Othello as somewhat unintelligent, more physical than cerebral. When Emilia has discovered Othello immediately after he has killed Desdemona, she cries out, "O thou dull Moor" (Act V, Sc. 2, 225) and adds, "What should such a *fool*/ Do with so good a woman?" Iago has made Othello act the part of a fool—a jealous fool. And this is one of the central equations worked out throughout the course of the play. Othello is particularly suited to lose his abilities to reason because he has always put a certain amount of faith in magic. We recall his explanation of the handkerchief to Desdemona:

> 'Tis true: there's magic in the web of it:
> A sibyl, that had number'd in the world
> The sun to course two hundred compasses,
> In her prophetic fury sew'd the work.　　(Act III, Sc. 4, 69-72)

Iago, on the other hand, frequently announces his confidence that wit can overpower magic, or, as he states in Act II, Scene 3: "Thou knows't we work by wit, and not by witchcraft;/ And wit depends on dilatory time." Thus the logic of the inducement of Othello to wrong action is easily understood in the thematic connection between jealousy and ignorance. And who is thus more fit to become jealous than the relatively unintellectual, literal Othello?

Question 13.
Is the theme of deception relatively conventional?

Answer
No. Shakespeare's development of Iago's deception of Othello has an unusual bent to it, inasmuch as Othello is a man easily convinced of literal or visible concepts. Because Othello has an unusually heroic past and has always distinguished himself honorably, he feels that all men are somehow honorable. In his extreme personal honesty he believes firmly in Iago's honesty; that is, Othello, unlike many men, believes that what he sees is true. Near the very end of the first act, Iago says of Othello:

> The Moor is of a free and open nature,
> That thinks men honest that but seem to be so,
> And will as tenderly be led by the nose
> As asses are.   (lines 405-408)

The phase "that but seem to be so" is the clue to the unique abilty of Othello to be fooled and, as we discussed in answering question 12, this is what is happening throughout the play. In any case, when Othello and Iago are discussing Michael Cassio, Iago reiterates this phrase once again:

Iago: For Michael Cassio, I dare be sworn I think that he is honest.

Othello: I think so too.

Iago: Men should be what they seem; or those that be not, would they might seem none!

Othello: Certain, men should be what they seem.

(Act III, Sc. 3, 124-128)

Othello, in other words, is a man who puts unusually great faith in what "seems" to be true; his sole demand for proof of Desdemona's unfaithfulness is something visible, the "ocular proof" as it is called. This is Othello's final criterion for establishing the truth and in this sense he is unusual. Thus the entire theme of deception is somewhat unconventional; in most cases, the deception would not be accomplished so easily. The combination of Othello's extreme literality and the demands of the play's other equations between jealousy and ignorance makes the presentation of the deception unusually simple.

Question 14.
Is the auxiliary problem of "reputation" logically connected to the behavior of Othello?

Answer

One of the dramatic conventions of the Elizabethan theatre, and of plays involving military people in particular, is the use of an established and familiar code of honor. Such a code of honor practically dicates that a character act in a certain way. As *Othello* is a "military" play—in the sense that it is located in Cyprus in preparation for a battle—it is thus not surprising to find in it a code of honor. All great soldiers—and that includes Othello, simply by definitions established in Act I—desire to act honorably and in so doing to protect their "reputation." Shakespeare deliberately introduces the auxiliary theme of reputation as a part or emblem of the conventional code of honour. Thus when Iago is first suggesting to Othello that Cassio may be false with Desdemona, he introduces the possible loss of reputation which could come to Othello. Iago says:

> Good name in man and woman, dear my lord,
> Is the immediate jewel of their souls:
> Who steals my purse steals trash; 'tis something, nothing;
> 'Twas mine, 'tis his, and has been slave to thousands;
> But he that filches from me my good name
> Robs me of that which not enriches him
> And makes me poor indeed.   (Act III, Sc. 3, 155-161)

Othello's fear of the loss of his honor is foreshadowed by Cassio's reaction to his demotion; Cassio, also a soldier and a man of honor, cries out that he is in agony over the loss of his reputation, making it clear to the audience that this convention is to operate in the play:

> Reputation, reputation, reputation! O, I have lost my reputation! I have lost the immortal part of myself, and what remains is bestial. My reputation, Iago, my reputation!
>
> (Act II, Sc. 3, 262-265)

That Shakespeare wants to make the point clear is evident in his repetition of the word "reputation" six times. Furthermore, this statement fixes the values in the world of *Othello*; "reputation" has connotations of "immortality" while all other considerations have a "bestial" association. The true irony is that Othello must act like a beast to protect his immortality.

Question 15.

To what extent is *Othello* concerned with innocence?

Answer

Desdemona is somehow almost unbelievable to us, and this may be due to her innocence. Our understanding of Desdemona is inhibited by her seeming duality: her sexuality and her naive ways. When she is first pleading to the Duke of Venice that she be allowed to accompany Othello to Cyprus, her argument is phrased in terms of her desire to be in the physical presence of Othello:

> That I did love the Moor to live with him,
> My downright violence and storm of fortunes
> May trumpet to the world: . . .
> So that, dear lords, if I be left behind,
> A moth of peace, and he go to the war,
> The rites for which I love him are bereft me,
> And I a heavy interim shall support
> By his dear absence. Let me go with him.   (lines 249-260)

Desdemona's desire to live with Othello and thus enjoy her conjugal rites is very understandable, particularly in light of her condition as a new bride. She is not sexually innocent, however, and this tends to confuse our general understanding of her as *the* innocent person in the play. Of course Cassio is innocent but our affections flow toward the helpless Desdemona; it is precisely because she is so helpless, as several critics have argued, that we are so moved by her even though we never feel that we know her that well.

When Desdemona is accused of being "false as hell" by Othello in Act IV, Scene 2, she is totally unable to understand what he means; she innocently suggests that he should not be mad at her if there is some distressing news from Venice. After he has called her a whore, she asks herself, "How have I been behaved, that he might stick/ The small'st opinion on my least misuse? (lines 108-109). When we soon see Desdemona begging from *Iago* advice on how to win back Othello, we seem to view her as the very personification of innocence; the mere fact that she addresses "good Iago" is such sad irony:

> O good Iago,
> What shall I do to win my lord again?
> Good friend, go to him; for, by this light of heaven,
> I know not how I lost him. Here I kneel:
> If e'er my will did trespass 'gainst his love,
> Either in discourse of thought or actual deed,
> Or that mine eyes, mine ears, or any sense,
> Delighted them in any other form;
> Or that I do not yet, and ever did,
> And ever will—though he do shake me off
> To beggarly divorcement—love him dearly,
> Comfort forswear me! Unkindness may do much;
> And his unkindness may defeat my life,
> But never taint my love.   (lines 148-161)

Thus is Desdemona completely unaware of the nature of Othello's anger. She prophetically notes her forthcoming murder, even though she does not understand why. This seems to be the epitome of her innocence: her willingness to die if Othello so decides, even without knowing why. And thus she has told Emilia to put the wedding sheets on the bed this night, and even instructed Emilia, "If I do die before thee, prithee shroud me/ In one of those same sheets" (Act IV, Sc. 3, 24-25). Then, finally, she is shown at the peak of innocence as she begins to sing the melancholy death-song, "willow."

As in her various suggestions that she would love Othello even up to and after her death, so her behaviour in the last act bears witness to her feelings. When Emilia discovers Desdemona after she has been smothered by Othello, she asks, "O, who hath done this deed?" Desdemona sighs, "Nobody; I myself. Farewell" (lines 123-124). This is true innocence; this pitiful destruction of innocence is part of the major action of the play. Just as Emilia's coarse "experienced" ways help us to appreciate, by contrast, Desdemona's innocent ways, so Desdemona's white purity of heart and soul make Othello's poisoned spirit that much more detestable. The play is primarily concerned with demonstrating the evil effects of jealousy; this is accomplished in more striking or dramatic terms by having the jealousy unfounded (as it so often is) and by having the object of jealousy so extremely loyal and innocent. Desdemona's pure love is so overpoweringly dramatized—to the final extent of her refusing to name Othello as her murderer—that we feel ourselves not simply revolted by jealousy and its ill effects, but even condemning the very possibility of jealousy in the world. The play, then, is about innocence only indirectly, only in its vivid contrast to distrust, suspicion, and jealousy, "the green-eyed monster."

Question 16.

Aside from the "code of honor" coloring, in what other ways is Othello defined by "conventions"?

Answer

To a certain extent, the meaning of the play is inherently and necessarily bound up in the depiction of the central character. Although we know that the play is about jealousy, and that we learn about jealousy through observing what happens to Othello and the other characters in the play, still we should at least describe the ways in which Shakespeare establishes Othello; what conventions are being used? As we have already mentioned, Othello "works" according to a code of honor and "reputation." This is evidence of his characterization as a *professional soldier*—a type or convention in many plays. In other words, as a professional soldier, Othello is easily introduced into the main fabric of the play. Then, when this is established—as it is in the picture of him as a valorous soldier and servant of the state in the first act—a second, more important "convention" takes command: Othello becomes the classical *tragic hero*, a good and "noble" man—as defined by Aristotle—who through some flaw is led to disaster and death. Othello's own flaw is his strong belief that things are what they seem; because of this flaw he is easily and rapidly convinced of Desdemona's guilt and is moved to swift disaster. In other words, the hero of the play fills the requirements of two conventions—the professional soldier, and the tragic hero. These conventions allow us to arrive at an understanding of Othello's temperament and behavior in a very short period of time; it is through the adherence to these conventions and their familiar meaning that Shakespeare is able to take us inside of Othello very swiftly.

Style

Methods of Analyzing Style

When we address ourselves to the problems of style, we are, in effect, addressing ourselves to a relatively large group of components rather than to a single entity. Style is the basic verbal presentation of ideas and, in particular, the ways in which one specified author or dramatist *chooses* to express his ideas. Under the heading of style we place such components as arrangement, diction, rhythm, emphasis, figurative language, imagery, abstractions, etc. The best place to begin, it would seem, is with a consideration of diction.

1. Diction

Diction is the choice of words in expressing ideas. The words themselves constitute what we term a "vocabulary," while diction has to do with how the words of this vocabulary are chosen. In John Knowles' well-known novel, *A Separate Peace*, for example, the diction is military: that is, ideas are expressed in terms of war and the vocabulary of war is employed. In *Macbeth*, there is a great deal of the vocabulary of witchcraft and many of the ideas are presented in terms suggestive of mystery and horror. Diction refers only to the selection of the words; the manner in which the author arranges them constitutes the essence of his particular style.

2. Imagery

In works of art we discover various "images" or representations of objects and people which somehow educate our senses. An image is a figure of speech employed in such a way that something comes to have a greater meaning than is implied in its literal sense. If throughout a play or a poem we find a linking between light and goodness, while at the same time we find an association of evil with darkness, we can then speak of the imagery of light and darkness. If many images of a similar nature are used we can begin to speak of various "patterns of imagery." For example, in Dickens' long novel *Bleak House*, every character is slowly associated with either an animal that is predatory or an animal which is meek and preyed upon. Thus we can speak of the imagery of hunting, or of imprisonment.

3. Figurative Language

An author places his own particular stamp on his work by employing figurative language. That is, the author communicates ideas to us by way of *analogies*. In a certain "figure" the poet presents one thing on the surface while very directly implying something else beneath the surface. The most common figures are the simile and the metaphor. In a simile, the poet or writer says that "X is *like* (or *as*) Y," while in a metaphor, the poet says "X is Y," in both cases hoping to increase our appreciation for something by showing us something analogous to it. "My love is a rose" is a metaphor which suggests to us the beauty and the developing freshness of love by associating love with a rose. Throughout most works of literature, we discover figures of speech, and, although metaphors and similes are the most common, the student should also acquaint himself with other figures such as "antithesis," "personification," "metonymy," "synecdoche," and "hyperbole."

4. Emphasis

The principle behind "emphasis" is simply that the writer should devote the right amount of attention to what is more important; that is, the time spent on certain ideas should correspond roughly to the importance of those ideas within the work. The sequence of presentation is important, but the main consideration is that the author does not spend a disproportionate amount of time on something trivial or, conversely, insufficient time on what is of major importance. Furthermore, when we consider emphasis as a component of an author's style, we should try to notice how detail is subordinated to the larger ideas. Put another way, we need to concentrate on the relationship of detail to what is universally implied. This leads us into a consideration of what is *general* and what is *particular*. We should single out some of the major statements of the theme, and then demonstrate their general truth by noting the ways in which particular statements support them.

5. Point of View

One aspect of style not discernible as easily in a play, but often of central importance to the understanding of a novel or a poem, is "point of view." We explain the attitude which the narrator or poet has toward his material. Further, what is the perspective of the poet? Is he writing about something in the past? If so, how far into the past? Is he sad about what happened? In short, by posing a series of questions we try to discover the writer's basic feelings behind the narration of the story; by explaining the position of the narrator we automatically describe the ways in which we can talk about a particular literary work.

6. Subjective Elements of Style

As style concerns the ways in which one particular author offers us a set of ideas, we must explain precisely what is particular about his methods. What are the private and personal feelings which shade all of the material? Is Shakespeare, for example, abnormally hateful of jealousy and is this hatred reflected in his style? Does the Author have an anti-feminism which can be seen evidenced in certain stylistic excesses? This leads to a final consideration.

7. Comparing to Style of Other Works by Same Author

Because we are interested primarily in making conclusions about the style of one particular work and not about the author, we should try to discover what is unique about the style of one of his works. By comparing the style of the work with which we are concerned with the style of other works by the same author, we can either make generalizations about the author's style, or else explain what is stylistically unique about the particular work in question.

Questions and Answers on Style

Question 17.

Is there appropriate "emphasis" on the theme of *Othello* or is Shakespeare's attention to jealousy excessive?

Answer

One of the stylistic devices in *Othello* is the way in which Shakespeare's presentation of jealousy is made almost equivalent to the emotion. In other words, jealousy is described throughout the play as a blistering monstrosity which becomes increasingly more destructive and increasingly intense. And as jealousy is always growing, so does Shakespeare's presentation of jealousy grow throughout the play. Shakespeare's attention to jealousy is only minimal in the opening act of the play, then in Act II moves swiftly to center stage and stays there for the duration of the play. Shakespeare is showing us the actual way in which jealousy itself becomes excessive by giving excessive treatment to jealousy in a variety of speeches — between Othello and Iago, Desdemona and Emilia, Othello and Desdemona, Emilia and Othello. In short, almost every pairing of the characters in the final acts of the play directs our attention to jealousy, so that we in the audience become as obsessed with the whole idea of jealousy as is Othello. Thus his intense reactions and his entire behavior seem more logical and even necessary. When Iago cautions Othello, "O, beware, my lord, of jealousy; / It is the green-eyed monster which doth mock / The meat it feeds on" (Act III, Sc. 3, 165-167), he is introducing an idea of jealousy which must necessarily continue in its enlargement throughout the play.

In the following scene, Emilia returns to the idea of jealousy as a monster, cautioning Desdemona, "'Tis a monster/ Begot upon itself, born on itself" (lines 161-162). Emilia has reminded us, as it were, of the nature of jealousy. The entire fabric of the play is slowly subordinated to the developing beast of jealousy, and we can not say that Shakespeare is any more excessive than the emotion itself; the demands of the presentation of jealousy are aptly met through an appropriate emphasis on jealousy in different parts of the play — low in the beginning and high in the end.

Question 18.

Explain the basic imagery of "magic" and "witchcraft" in *Othello*. How does this imagery relate to Othello's manner of speaking?

Answer

As Robert B. Heilman first pointed out, there is a sharp dichotomy between wit and witchcraft throughout *Othello*; we see an association of magic and bizarre supernaturalism in Othello and in his love for Desdemona, while at the same time we see the opposition to this magic presented in the form of wit: in particular, in the form of Iago's scheming malice. In accordance with the demands of this central polarization, it is not surprising that we find various references to magic in the images of the play. The central magic of the play is linked to Othello's marriage to Desdemona. When Brabantio first learns that his daughter Desdemona has eloped with the Moor, he immediately accuses Othello of enchanting her (Act I, Sc. 2, 63 ff.). When Othello is through with his explanation of how they honorably fell in love, he says wryly, "This only is the witchcraft I have used" (Act I, Sc. 3, 169). In these early suggestions associating Othello with witchcraft is an essential implication that black people are somehow allied with supernatural or even unnatural abilities; Othello's image becomes that of a kind of would-be black sorcerer. He is, after all, from a different background, and in his minority poses a threat to the understanding of the others. When Othello explains to Desdemona that there is magic in the web of the handkerchief (Act III, Sc. 4, 69 ff.), he is telling the audience that there is a certain magic both in his relationship to Desdemona and in the entire play. The entire legend of the handkerchief — that she who loses it will lose her husband — is borne out by the action of the play. And when Desdemona herself says, "Sure, there's some wonder in this handkerchief" (Act III, Sc. 4, 101), we realize that she too believes in the magic and thus in the legend.

Because of the way in which Othello is associated with magic through the imagery, and primarily through the handkerchief, he speaks in a less "witty" way than the opposition. Othello himself draws attention to his plain speech in the first act: "Rude am I in my speech, / And little bless'd with the soft phrase of peace" (lines 81-82). Often we are reminded that Othello can only speak in a fundamental way, and thus there is an association between his charm and his verbal weakness. Believing in magic as he does, it is unnecessary for him to have cultivated excellent speech. When he realizes in the end of the play that he has been tricked, he feels certain that Iago is a real devil and thus incapable of being killed; this statement testifies to his superstition. And, finally, when he asks to be punished, he speaks in terms of a demonic destruction: he asks devils to whip him away and, further, that he be roasted in sulphur — he asks, in other words, for a quasi-magical death. He has been the victim of a peculiar magic, he feels, from the very beginning; how else can he explain to himself that he has erred in slaying his wife?

Question 19.

What are some of the other patterns of imagery in *Othello*?

Answer

The central pattern of imagery, one closely connected at times to the ideas of magic and witchcraft, is that of imprisonment, of evil entrapping good, of Iago the spider catching Othello the fly. In Brabantio's early accusations he refers to a possible set of "chains of magic" which Othello must have used to ensnare Desdemona. The irony is that Iago is the one trying to wrap Othello in the chains of jealousy. When Cassio is seen to take Desdemona's hand, Iago turns to the audience in an aside and says, *"With as little a web as this will I ensnare as great a fly as Cassio"* (Act II, Sc. 1, 169-170). This image of ensnarement is maintained throughout the play. Later Iago explains how he will use Desdemona's pleas to Othello to be kind to Cassio as a net in which to ensnare Othello:

> So will I turn her virtue into pitch,
> And out of her own goodness make the net
> That shall enmesh them all.   (Act II, Sc. 3, 366-368)

Iago's busy plans to enmesh Othello in a net lead the audience to an appreciation of Shakespeare's marvelous irony every time Othello says that he is "bound" to Iago, as for example in Act III, Scene 3, where Othello says to Iago, "I am bound to thee for ever" (line 213). This acquires further irony when Iago himself says that he is the one who is "bound" to Othello, as in "I am your own for ever" (line 480). There is a web in which Othello is being trapped, and thus the irony is further broadened when he talks about the magic in the "web" of the handkerchief.

Iago is gleefully proud of his attempts to enmesh Othello and is frequently seen laughing evilly on the sidelines whenever he thinks his traps are working as in Act IV, Scene 1, when he says:

> Work on,
> My medicine work! Thus credulous fools are *caught*;
> And many worthy and chaste dames even thus,
> All guiltless, meet reproach.   (lines 45-48)

In the last act, after Othello has killed the innocent Desdemona and then learned of her innocence, he turns in agony and quietly asks that someone explain to him why he has been "ensnared" in such an evil way: "Demand that demi-devil/ *Why he hath thus ensnared my soul and body*" (lines 301-302). This is the final utterance within the pattern of ensnarement which has been operative throughout the play. Shakespeare has relied on a fairly conventional analogy of the spider and the fly to represent the way in which evil ruins good, but Shakespeare's development of the analogy is expert and just subtle enough to remain artistic and creative in spite of this conventional picture.

A final pattern of imagery is that of chiaroscuro, the designation we have for the contrasts of black and white. There is an easily identified symbolism in Othello's blackness, which will be destructive, and Desdemona's whiteness, which represents her innocence and purity. When Desdemona is first described by Cassio to the officers awaiting her arrival at Cyprus, she is considered to be beyond description, "one that excels the quirks of blazoning pens" and, further, she is "divine" and "the grace of heaven" (Act II, Sc. 1, 60 ff.). Throughout the play we are conscious of Desdemona's pale white skin and the way in which that paleness suggests divinity and innocence. At the same time, Othello talks about his black face and others refer to his blackness; the images make Othello something of a gathering dark storm which will burst upon the whiteness or goodness of Desdemona.

Question 20.

Discuss Shakespeare's diction and use of figurative language in *Othello*.

Answer

Shakespeare's diction in the play is designed to develop characterization through manner of speech. Each character's choice of words tells us something about him. Othello admits in simple terms that he is not an elegant speaker and his vocabulary, for the most part, is that of the warrior. When Othello has decided to punish Desdemona for her supposed unfaithfulness with Cassio, Othello shouts to Iago: "I will chop her into messes" (Act IV, Sc. 1, 211). The words are those of the man described early in the play by Iago as a "barbarian." Cassio's language, similarly, presents him as a faithful officer but, at times, a lover of the whore Bianca. Emilia speaks as the experienced wife and woman; she speaks in a coarse way, particularly when explaining her pessimistic view of men and their feelings about women. For example, she explains to the innocent Desdemona:

> 'Tis not a year or two shows us a man:
> They are all but stomachs, and we all but food;
> They eat us hungerly, and when they are full,
> They belch us.   (Act III, Sc. 4, 103-106)

Each character is given a manner of expression and a particular vocabulary which will best help the audience see clearly the essence of that character. Iago is the most consistently portrayed through his long, villainous, sensuous speeches, as, for example, at the end of Act II:

> How am I then a villain
> To counsel Cassio to this parallel course,
> Directly to his good? Divinity of hell!
> When devils will the blackest sins put on,
> They do suggest at first with heavenly shows,
> As I do now: for whiles this honest fool
> Plies Desdemona to repair his fortunes,
> And she for him pleads strongly to the Moor,
> I'll pour this pestilence into his ear,
> That she repeals him for her body's lust;
> And by how much she strives to do him good,
> She shall undo her credit with the Moor.   (lines 354-365)

Iago's speech is very typical here, particularly in the line, "I'll pour this pestilence into his ear." Here we find Shakespeare using a figure of speech, a hyperbole — that is, an exaggeration. Literally, Iago will pour nothing into Othello's ear; what he will do is offer Othello some malicious gossip. And this is the way the language of the play "works"; everything is said in figurative fashion, made dramatic through new expressions. Again and again, through metaphors, similes, and hyperboles, Shakespeare relies heavily on figurative speech.

A final stylistic consideration to be noted is illustrated by Iago's long speech which we have just examined. Like so many of the speeches in the play, it is written in what we call *blank verse,* unrhyming iambic pentameter; we can scan the lines easily, for each has five poetic feet, with each foot containing an unstressed syllable followed by a stressed one: "I'll pour/this pes/tilence/into/his ear." The expert use of blank verse is one of Shakespeare's outstanding contributions to dramatic language, for the rhythm and cadence become hypnotic as the stressed syllables alternate.

Othello: A Tragedy of Jealousy

In *Othello* Shakespeare presents us with the tragic spectacle of a man who, in a spirit of jealous rage, destroys what he loves best in all the world. Such a spectacle must of necessity be painful, whatever the object destroyed and whoever the destroyer, but it is doubly painful and deeply tragic when we see an essentially noble man brutally killing his pure, faithful and loving young wife in the mistaken belief that she is a strumpet.

Clearly, if this tragedy is to make its full impact, we must envisage the marriage of Othello and Desdemona as a real 'marriage of true minds', a deep love based on a mutual awareness, and a true appreciation, of each other's worth, a love that has in it none of the element of sensual lust that characterized the relationship of Claudius and Gertrude or Troilus and Cressida. Thus Desdemona affirms:

> I saw Othello's visage in his mind,
> And to his honours and his valiant parts
> Did I my soul and fortunes consecrate . . .   (Act I, Sc. 3, 253)

while Othello himself reassures the Venetian council that he desires Desdemona's presence in Cyprus

>   . . . not
> To please the palate of my appetite,
> Nor to comply with heat — the young affects
> In me defunct — and proper satisfaction,
> But to be free and bounteous to her mind: (Act I, Sc. 3, 262)

The love of Othello and Desdemona is a love that transcends the physical barriers of colour, nationality and age. Its tenderness and passion are evident whenever they speak about each other or their unconventional courtship in the first part of the play, before Iago's insinuations have begun to affect the hero. Othello won his 'gentle' Desdemona by relating to her the adventures and dangers he had experienced:

> She loved me for the dangers I had pass'd,
> And I loved her that she did pity them.   (Act I, Sc. 3, 167)

His adoration of Desdemona is vividly brought out in their ecstatic reunion at Cyprus:

> . . . O my soul's joy!
> If after every tempest comes such calms,
> May the winds blow till they have waken'd death!
> And let the labouring bark climb hills of seas
> Olympus-high and duck again as low
> As hell's from heaven! If it were now to die,
> 'Twere now to be most happy; for, I fear,
> My soul hath her content so absolute
> That not another comfort like to this
> Succeeds in unknown fate.   (Act II, Sc. 1, 187)

Or we may note the fondness and tenderness, as well as the ominously prophetic note, of:

> Excellent wretch! Perdition catch my soul,
> But I do love thee! and when I love thee not,
> Chaos is come again.   (Act III, Sc. 3, 89)

Yet, despite the way in which the purity and depth of their love is ultimately conveyed in the last scene of Act I, throughout Act II and at the opening of Act III, it is significant that the marriage is presented quite differently at the opening of the play, when Iago and Roderigo rouse Brabantio from his sleep to inform him of his daughter's elopement.

> Even now, now very now, an old black ram
> Is tupping your white ewe . . .

> . . . the devil will make a grandsire of you:
> . . . you'll have your daughter covered with a Barbary horse;
> you'll have your nephews neigh to you; you'll have coursers
> for cousins and gennets for germans.   (Act I, Sc. 1, 87)

Thus speaks Iago, stressing the bestiality and animalism of the relationship which stem from Othello's grossness. Roderigo assures Brabantio that his fair daughter has been 'transported' (and we must remember that, in addition to the literal meaning, the word connotes 'bewitched') 'To the gross clasp of a lascivious Moor'. Desdemona

> . . . hath made a gross revolt;
> Tying her duty, beauty, wit and fortunes
> In an extravagant and wheeling stranger
> Of here and every where . . .   (Act I, Sc. 1, 135)

Nor is it only the meaner minds of Iago and Roderigo, who have already been firmly established as petty and envious at the very beginning of Scene I, that hold this view of the marriage. Even Brabantio alleges that only foul witchcraft could have led Desdemona to betray her birth, her breeding, her very nature, so far as to marry the black monster, Othello.

> O thou foul thief, where hast thous stow'd
>   my daughter?
> Damn'd as thou art, thou hast enchanted her;
> For I'll refer me to all things of sense,
> If she in chains of magic were not bound,
> Whether a maid so tender, fair and happy,
> So opposite to marriage that she shunn'd
> The wealthy curled darlings of our nation,
> Would ever have, to incur a general mock,
> Run from her guardage to the sooty bosom
> Of such a thing as thou, to fear, not to delight.
> Judge me the world, if 'tis not gross in sense
> That thou hast practised on her with foul charms,
> Abused her delicate youth with drugs or minerals
> That weaken motion: I'll have't disputed on;
> 'Tis probable and palpable to thinking.
> I therefore apprehend and do attach thee
> For an abuser of the world, a practiser
> Of arts inhibited and out of warrant.   (Act I, Sc. 2, 62)

He tells the Duke that Desdemona

> . . . is abused, stol'n from me, and corrupted
> By spells and medicines bought of mountebanks;
> For nature so preposterously to err,
> Being not deficient, blind, or lame of sense,
> Sans witchcraft could not.   (Act I, Sc. 3, 60)

104

Thus the disparity and apparent bestiality and unnaturalness of the match, together with the horror and revulsion it arouses in some, at least, of the Venetian citizens, are most vividly brought out. It is significant that Othello is not even referred to by name until the Duke greets him halfway through Scene 3; until then he is called 'the Moor', 'the thick-lips', 'the Devil' and a number of similar unflattering terms. His blackness and the feelings of hatred, revulsion and disgust that this arouses, most particularly when he is thought of in relation to a white woman, are what Shakespeare seeks to impress us with at the very beginning of the play and he does this because the fact that Othello is a Moor and a foreigner in Venice is as important in this play as the fact that Shylock is a Jew was important to *The Merchant of Venice*. Shakespeare wants to impress upon us at the very outset how easily tenable an unfavourable view of the marriage is, particularly by those meaner minds who fail to perceive Othello's greatness and Desdemona's purity. To many Venetians Desdemona's self-acknowledged 'downright violence' in marrying Othello seems unnatural and preposterous, explicable only by a diseased will on her part or witchcraft on his.

It is precisely because of the apparent, obvious, incongruity of the marriage that Iago is able to persuade even Othello himself of the abnormality of Desdemona's behaviour in preferring him to

> . . . many proposed matches
> Of her own clime, complexion, and degree,
> Whereto we see in all things nature tends —   (Act III, Sc. 3, 229)

With the uttermost audacity he goes on to point out that these same lustful desires that have led Desdemona to marry Othello may yet, in time, be overruled by her reasonable judgement so that, in wiser mood, comparing him with her own countrymen, she may well repent her unsuitable marriage. So cogent is Iago's argument that Othello, left alone on the stage, also contemplates the physical and cultural disparity between himself and his wife:

> . . . Haply, for I am black
> And have not those soft parts of conversation
> That chambers have, or for I am declined
> Into the vale of years, — yet that's not much —
> She's gone. I am abused; and my relief
> Must be to loathe her . . .   (Act III, Sc. 3, 263)

He assumes that his own lack of the qualities she is accustomed to in the young men about her may well have led to her infidelity.

Thus Iago plays upon Othello's awareness of his own foreignness in order to arouse his suspicions against Desdemona. But he also, as a native of Venice, undertakes to guide and advise Othello in the customs of Venetian society, telling him that all Venetian wives are faithless:

> I know our country disposition well;
> In Venice they do let heaven see the pranks

They dare not show their husbands; their best conscience
Is not to leave't undone, but keep't unknown.

(Act III, Sc. 3, 201)

To this information Othello responds with the credulous 'Dost thou say so?' which marks his readiness to believe the 'expert' Iago, a readiness which stems solely from Othello's awareness of his own foreignness, not only to the ways of Venice but to the customs and habits of peacetime existence:

> . . . little of this great world can I speak,
> More than pertains to feats of broil and battle.

(Act I, Sc. 3, 86)

Othello is portrayed as a great and noble warrior of royal descent. He is a man of action who is truly at home only on the battlefields on which his life has been spent since the age of seven. The speed with which he acts, once his decision is made, is illustrated by the way in which he deals with the midnight riot that leads to the dummary dismissal of Cassio. When Iago begins his accusation of Desdemona, Othello plans to deal with her in his usual way:

> I'll see before I doubt; when I doubt, prove;
> And on the proof, there is no more but this, —
> Away at once with love or jealousy!   (Act III, Sc. 3, 190)

The self-confidence in his own capacity for judgement which he reveals in these lines is wholly consistent with the pride and self-esteem he displays throughout the first part of the play: it is a self-confidence bred and justified by years of glorious military leadership, but even in the dismissal of Cassio we are shown that Othello is not a very good judge of human character. He is misled by appearances and, just as his 'free and open nature' leads him to 'think men honest that but seem to be so', so conversely he also judges evil by outer appearance alone.

Playing on Othello's self-avowed reliance on appearances in determining his actions, Iago supplies him with the visible, tangible proof of Desdemona's adultery with Cassio that he desires. But once again, as in so many others of his plays, Shakespeare stresses how false and misleading appearances can be. Nowhere else in any of the tragedies are there so many episodes in which the audience is informed of the truth while the hero remains ignorant, blinded by appearances which we know to be wholly, and often deliberately, misleading. It is, in fact, mainly this intense use of dramatic irony that is responsible for the impression of stupidity that Othello so often makes upon an audience; because *we* are taken into Iago's confidence and forewarned of all his cunning schemes to trap his fellows, we expect a similar awareness of what appears so self-evident on the part of the other characters of the play. The episode of the handkerchief and that of the conversation concerning Bianca, which Othello believes to be about Desdemona, are but two of the incidents in which Iago tricks Othello into believing the evidence of his eyes and ears to be infallible confirmation of Desdemona's wantonness. As in *Troilus and Cressida*, reason is overthrown by the passion which is aroused as a result of placing trust in appearances that prove to be false. However great Othello may be as a soldier, he lacks the reasonable judgement essential to the Complete Man. The overriding importance of reason is stressed, ironically enough, by none other than Iago:

> . . .If the balance of our lives had not one scale of
> reason to poise another of sensuality, the blood and
> baseness of our natures would conduct us to most
> preposterous conclusions: but we have reason to cool
> our raging motions, our carnal stings, our unbitted
> lusts, . . .   (Act I, Sc. 3, 330)

The major dramatic action of the play shows us the way in which the passion of jealousy, which derives from pride and breeds anger, gradually gains control over Othello and destroys his initial nobility, so that he finally turns into the black beast that he was at first unjustly accused of being. The decline in the moral and spiritual stature of Othello goes hand in hand with the destruction of his love for and faith in Desdemona. From the ecstasy of their reunion at Cyprus, where the calm rhythm of the verse corresponds to the equilibrium in Othello's mind, we proceed to the impatience with which, immediately after Iago's insinuations have begun to work upon him, he pushes aside the little handkerchief with which Desdemona offers to bind his aching forehead. Already his reason is undermined. The poison of Iago's 'dangerous conceits' is already working and the villain confidently prophecies:

> Not poppy, nor mandragora,
> Nor all the drowsy syrups of the world,
> Shall ever medicine thee to that sweet sleep
> Which thou owedst yesterday.   (Act III, Sc. 3, 330)

The 'green-eyed monster' jealousy is already 'mocking the meat it feeds on; calm of mind and self-confidence disappear as the great general gives way to the jealous husband:

> . . .O, now, for ever
> Farewell the tranquil mind! farewell content!
> Farewell the plumed troop, and the big wars,
> That make ambition virtue! O, farewell!
> Farewell the neighing steed, and the shrill trump,
> The spirit-stirring drum, the ear-piercing fife,
> The royal banner, and all quality,
> Pride, pomp and circumstance of glorious war!
> And, O you mortal engines, whose rude throats
> The immortal Jove's dread clamours counterfeit,
> Farewell! Othello's occupation's gone!   (Act III, Sc. 3, 347)

The anger and persistence with which Othello demands her handkerchief frighten Desdemona into panicky lying and lead her to wondering comment on the alteration in her husband: 'My lord is not my lord, nor should I know him/ Were he in favour as in humour altered'. The decline to bestiality is dramatically brought out in the next scene (Act IV, Sc. 1), where Iago's half-hints, innuendos and unfinished sentences rouse Othello to such a pitch of jealous passion that he falls grovelling in an epileptic trance. By the end of this scene, having witnessed Iago's exchange with Cassio about Bianca and seen Desdemona's handkerchief in the hands of this strumpet, his mind is made up and he determines to avenge the wrong Desdemona has done to his honour. Yet even as he plans her death his better judgement struggles to reassert itself, battling with his jealous passion:

> Ay, let her rot, and perish, and be damned to-night; for she
> shall not live: no, my heart is turned to stone; I strike it, and it
> hurts my hand. O, the world hath not a sweeter creature: she
> might lie by an emperor's side and command him tasks.
>
> (Act IV, Sc. 1, 191)

He contemplates Desdemona's physical and mental perfections but Iago's appeals to his wounded honour and his sense of vengeance win the day. When Iago advises him to 'strangle her in her bed, even the bed she hath contaminated', Othello gloats upon the appropriateness of the punishment: 'Good, good. The justice of it pleases. Very good.' The perversion which underlies this conception of justice is obvious. A few minutes later he strikes Desdemona in public and behaves with such astonishing violence that the newly-arrived Lodovico exclaims wonderingly: 'This would not be believed in Venice.' The great change that has come over Othello is what so appals the onlookers:

> Is this the noble Moor whom our full senate
> Call all in all sufficient? Is this the nature
> Whom passion could not shake? whose solid virtue
> The shot of accident, nor dart of chance,
> Could neither graze nor pierce?   (Act IV, Sc. 1, 275)

In Act IV, Scene 2, Othello's loathing and contempt for Desdemona find their expression in his treating her like a whore and Emilia as their bawd. It is interesting to note that Othello, in this case, rejects the evidence of appearances, just as Troilus at first rejected the visual evidence he had always previously relied upon, when he saw the infidelity of Cressida. With tragic irony, Othello rejects appearances as false on the single occasion when they are, in fact, an excellent indication of the reality that underlies them. It is in this scene that Othello claims that he could endure with stoic patience all ills that the Heavens might impose upon him save his wife's infidelity:

> . . . Turn thy complexion there,
> Patience, thou young and rose-lipp'd cherubin,—
> Ay, there, look grim as hell!   (Act IV, Sc. 2, 62)

As in Hamlet, revenge and Hell-are associated and even equated. Though Othello claims that he is executing an act of divine justice, the scene of her murder (like the final scene of Hamlet) brings out clearly the fact that an act of revenge is not an act of calm and reasoned justice but an expression of violent and selfish passion. In the soliloquy which opens the final scene Othello is still in a state of conflict, the purity and beauty of the sleeping Desdemona battling with his vengeful passions and almost overruling the 'cause' which motivates him, that 'cause' which he may not name to the 'chaste stars'. When Desdemona wakes, Othello speaks to her at first in the calm tones of the 'official' executioner, bidding her pray and confess her crimes so that she may go purified to her death: 'I would not kill thy unprepared spirit./ No, Heaven forfend! I would not kill thy soul'. But as she pleads with him 'bloody passion shakes [his] frame'. Her denials of his accusations and allegations concerning Cassio and the handkerchief carry no weight with him, for to counter her denials he has the visible proof he had demanded of Iago when he bade him: 'Villain, be sure thou prove my love a whore,/ Be sure of it, give me the ocular proof'. He counters her denials with the firm assertion 'By Heaven, I saw my handkerchief in's hand. . .I saw the handkerchief.' His anger mounts rapidly until finally he murders 'the strumpet' without giving her the opportunity for 'one prayer'. His heart has been turned to stone and that which he 'thought a sacrifice' is, indeed, brutal murder.

Urged on by a misconception of honour that is engendered by his own sinful pride and self-esteem, which in their turn engender a murderous jealousy, Othello permits the passion of revenge to overwhelm his reasonable judgement and noble instincts, which tell him that Desdemona, despite all 'ocular proof' to the contrary, is pure and innocent. Yet in this tragedy the responsibility for the tragic outcome does not lie solely with the hero. It is Iago who is responsible for the devilish misrepresentation which so fatally deceives Othello. The whole terrible plot is engineered by this super-subtle villain whose greatest triumph lies in the way in which he succeeds in convincing all those with whom he has dealings that he is 'honest and loving'. To us alone does he reveal the full extent of his devilish machinations; all his schemes are plotted aloud in soliloquy and, as I have already said, much of the horror of the tragedy stems from the way in which our apprehensions are fulfilled as we see one character after another succumbing to Iago's persuasiveness and hypocritical charm and falling straight into the trap he has set for them. Nor does his success seem as incredible and theatrically unreal as that of Richard III. Like that earlier Machiavellian, Iago plays upon the inherent weaknesses and passions in all his victims, but he does it all in the most credible way, as he himself points out, 'suggest[ing] at first with heavenly shows' in order ultimately to put on 'the blackest sins'.

The only aspect of Iago's actions that has given pause for thought is the apparent lack of motivation. But in fact Iago, like Othello, is motivated by the same envy and jealousy that arouse murderous hatred. We see this first in the opening scene, in which he expresses venomous contempt, anger and hatred at the fact that Cassio rather than himself has been appointed Othello's lieutenant. The wild envy and jealousy are evident later, too, when he begins his plotting:

> That Cassio loves her, I do well believe it;
> That she loves him, 'tis apt and of great credit:
> The Moor, howbeit that I endure him not,
> Is of a constant, loving, noble nature,
> And I dare think he'll prove to Desdemona
> A most dear husband. Now, I do love her too;
> Not out of absolute lust, though peradventure
> I stand accountant for as great a sin,
> But partly led to diet my revenge,
> For that I do suspect the lusty Moor
> Hath leap'd into my seat; the thought whereof
> Doth, like a poisonous mineral, gnaw my inwards;
> And nothing can or shall content my soul
> Till I am even'd with him, wife for wife,
> Or failing so, yet that I put the Moor
> At least into a jealousy so strong
> That judgement cannot cure. Which thing to do,
> If this poor trash of Venice, whom I trash
> For his quick hunting, stand the putting on,
> I'll have our Michael Cassio on the hip,
> Abuse him to the Moor in the rank garb—
> For I fear Cassio with my night-cap too—
> Make the Moor thank me, love me and reward me,
> For making him egregiously an ass
> And practising upon his peace and quiet
> Even to madness. 'Tis here, but yet confused:
> Knavery's plain face is never seen till used.   (Act II, Sc. 1, 295)

Envy of Cassio, jealousy of Othello's possession of Desdemona, jealous fear that both Othello and Cassio may have cuckolded him, and, of course, the incessant desire for money and power, the driving ambition to master others, all these lead Iago on to vindictively destructive action. He is like Milton's Satan, unable to bear the sight of others happier than himself. His jealousy is more horrible than that of Othello because Iago is altogether a meaner creature, wholly incapable of the nobility of thought and action that characterise the Othello of the play's opening acts. Iago could never claim, as Othello does, 'For naught I did in hate, but all in honour.' Indeed he confesses at the beginning of the play, 'I hate the Moor.' It is hatred alone that motivates him and the hatred is the natural outcome of a jealous, envious spirit.

The resemblance to Satan is explicitly stated. Iago is referred to as a 'demi-devil', 'a Devil', 'a viper' — he is the Snake in Eden, that persuades Man to commit the one act that will lead to his loss of Paradise. And the Paradise here is none other than Desdemona herself, as her character, her behaviour, the references to her and the imagery of the play clearly bring out. She is angelic in appearance, fair-haired, pure-complexioned, 'tender, fair and happy', so innocent and chaste that she cannot bring herself to utter the word 'whore' or to believe that there are indeed women who would betray their husbands.

> Tempests themselves, high seas and howling winds,
> The gutter'd rocks and congregated sands,—
> Traitors ensteep'd to clog the guiltless keel,—
> As having sense of beauty, do omit
> Their mortal natures, letting go safely by
> The divine Desdemona. (Act II, Sc. 1, 68)

She looks like 'one of Heaven' and the devils may fear to seize her. As he contemplates her sleeping figure, Othello, even on the verge of killing her for unchastity, compares her to all the symbols of perfection: snow, alabaster, the rose. She is 'the cunning'st pattern of excelling nature', the most beautiful model-form devised by Nature as a pattern for forming other creatures. Her breath is 'balmy' and her soul is the 'Promethean fire', derived from Heaven. Yet Othello in his self-confidence and wounded pride, deceived by the super-subtle, wily, scheming Iago, murders her. The symbolism is quite explicit as the perplexed Othello, aware at last of his fatal error, begs of those around him 'Will you, I pray, demand that demidevil/ Why he hath thus ensnared my soul and body?'

Yet the ultimate effect of the play, despite its highly naturalistic and painful theme, is one which reaffirms man's dignity and essential greatness. In committing the supposed act of justice Othello has in fact committed a brutal murder and thus brought upon himself not only that very dishonour and shame in this world from which the '*execution*' was intended to save him but also damnation in the world to come:

> . . .O ill-starr'd wench!
> Pale as thy smock! when we shall meet at compt,
> This look of thine will hurl my soul from heaven,
> And fiends will snatch at it. (Act V, Sc. 2, 272)

It is a perfect example of tragic reversal. But in his final speech all Othello's initial honour is restored. The final speech expresses self-knowledge, awareness, penitent regret for his sinful error. It leads, finally, to his passing judgement and executing punishment upon himself just as he had earlier, mistakenly, presumed to judge and execute Desdemona. Though Othello's '*greatness of heart*', his magnanimity, is here reasserted and he is once more the great soldier of Acts I and II it is surely significant that Shakespeare chooses this moment at which to stress once again Othello's foreignness.

...Set you down this;
And say besides, that in Aleppo once,
Where a malignant and a turban'd Turk
Beat a Venetian and traduced the state,
I took by the throat the circumcised dog,
And smote him, thus.   (Act V, Sc. 2, 351)

Though, in recalling the episode at Aleppo, Othello reminds the bystanders of the service he has rendered the Venetian state we may note that in finally smiting his own breast Othello equates *himself* with the 'circumcised dog' who had 'Beat a Venetian and traduced the state'. We are, as it were, back at the beginning, at the opening scenes which, as we saw, seemed designed specifically to stress the foreignness of Othello. On Iago may fall the main responsibility for the evil committed by Othello, but had Othello not been a foreigner, a stranger and outsider, at once tolerated yet suspect, outwardly confident yet inwardly intensely insecure, the poisonous seeds sown by Iago might have fallen on less fertile soil and borne no fatal fruit. In reading the play we must never forget what, in the theatre, is constantly clearly before our eyes—that this is the tragedy of Othello, the *Moor* of Venice.

By Alice Shalvi, *The World & Art of Shakespeare*, Israel Universities Press, 1967.

Othello Reconsidered

Othello is sometimes said to be Shakespeare's most perfect, most typical tragedy. It behooves us to inquire what is meant by this.

In the beginning of such an inquiry certain elementary facts stand out. Shakespeare's tragedy is a tragedy of blood, violence, and revenge. His age called for such a tragedy and his tradition dictated it. In this kind of tragedy death was the only acceptable end. Perhaps this feature was merely Senecan tradition; perhaps it arose from the fear of death entertained in Shakespeare's time and long before. Death was indeed of common occurrence. Man strove not so much to live as to avoid death. The theology of the age held out horrid spectacles of a life of torment after death. There seems little reason to doubt that Shakespeare and his contemporaries believed in the existence of perfect villains, children of the devil, not children of God. This belief underlies the destruction of heretics and witches. In our age we sometimes doubt whether there exists a human being who steadily, persistently, and naturally desires evil. But the villainy of Elizabethan villains was a force in the world.

Such belief in absolute villainy could have been readily enough derived from Seneca but seems to have established itself on the Elizabethan stage with Marlowe's Barabas in *The Jew of Malta*. Plenty of villains had made their appearance in romantic drama before Marlowe, but he introduced the code of complete villainy with his first Machiavel. Kyd's Lorenzo in *The Spanish Tragedy* is also a Machiavel, and he has sometimes been thought earlier than Barabas. The point is that these absolute villains differ from ordinary villains in their lack of any conflict between will and conscience. But they stand somewhat apart from romantic tragedy, and it remains to be decided whether, apart perhaps from Aaron, Shakespeare has any villain of completely evil character.

Again the Elizabethans held traditionally the view that tragedy might achieve sufficient dignity and importance to be worthy of treatment only when it concerned persons of high estate—as kings, princes, great prelates, noblemen, and heroes. The modern world has learned, in part through Ibsen, that the mere fact of being a man has in it sufficient import to achieve a tragic level of dignity and consequence. Modern fiction has taught the world much about the omnipresent possibility of tragedy. The Elizabethans probably knew this also, but without realizing it as a doctrine and practice. There was greatness and breadth in the Elizabethan point of view. To them, the greatest of them, the phenomenal world was a small and alien thing, and nature was subject to time and change. Philosophy could not then be approached through science, since no reliance was placed on the senses. Philosophy must be sought at the throne of God, in the stars, or in the pages of the wise men of the ancient world. Stoicism, which is not so much a philosophy as an exaltation of fortitude, was resorted to by the later Elizabethans as a sort of insurance against calamity. A certain haughtiness and sense of superiority to the multitude mark the Renaissance stoics. The Elizabethans exemplified, but probably rarely held as a conscious doctrine, the ideal of what we may call success in failure, although perhaps in true tragedy there is always a final note of triumph, sometimes of enlightenment, sometimes of repentance, sometimes of admiration for fortitude and virtue.

As a basis for the study of *Othello*, let us consider the following summary of Shakespearean tragedy, based in part on the work of a distinguished scholar, the late Professor R.M. Alden: Shakespeare inherited a crude tragedy of blood, but developed through the treatment of such stories as those of Romeo and Juliet and King Richard II an interest in the possibly tragic results of character and the inner life. He accepted the current belief in the possibility of human fiendishness, which he developed into terrible malignancy; and yet it is an open question whether he ever goes so far as to rob his villains of their human status. He found elements of tragedy in weakness, inefficiency, and defect of character as well as in positive tragic guilt. He made full use of the tragic backgrounds of life which appear in accident, untoward birth, and inescapable fate; but he never abandoned his faith in the human will, which is always allowed to play a part. He frequently lifts his defeated characters to a point where they may be said to defeat defeat. In his later work, as in *Othello*, he saw deeply into human nature and in terms of the psychology of his time presented terrific struggles of man against his own passions.

In *Othello*, a tragedy written probably in 1604, Shakespeare faced the cruelty and mystery of human life—power, passion, craft, elemental forces—greater things than man. Man's orderly habits are seen to be precarious. We even fear that character is not destiny. Othello suffers from his virtues. He is not jealous by nature, and his sudden attack is bolstered up by a psychology which we might call incredible if the news did not give us daily records of just such unexpected obsessions. The Elizabethans plainly believed because of their mechanistic physiological psychology that every man was a potential Othello. Othello is a colossal hero, sure of pre-eminence when in repose, but as terrible as an earthquake when disturbed. He is a romantic hero, a warrior, a traveler, and a leader of men. We see his life crowned with the glory of love. His is an elemental, simple nature. He has lived by faith alone, his faith has eventuated in love, and it is the wreck of the two that is his tragedy. Some critics have thought that his fall is rationally an impossibility and have argued that we have in the play a mere convention of the "calumniator believed," that Iago had to be believed in order that we might have a play. But this view needs qualification by the ancient idea of the effects of the evil counselor. In narrative the prince or high person is set upon a pedestal and glorified. He, as God's vicegerent, is untouchable. As soon as he becomes culpable, he forfeits our sympathy. Blame must be transferred from him to those who mislead him. Othello is presented as a great and good person largely by his wonderful speeches in the senate house and by the respect that is everywhere shown him, so that it is Iago who is to blame. This is true in literary convention and in actuality.

Iago has been selected and constructed for the ruin of Othello. Iago is a soldier with a soldier's discipline and the cunning that comes to a soldier in camp and field in getting the best for himself, in insisting on his rights, and in the manipulation of his superior officers. He has a superficial good nature and is careful of the practical value of reputation. He is possessed of cold selfishness and great powers of intellect and will but not of imagination. His is the creed of the ego. He has unexpectedly little positive ill will. He has spite only against anything that might weaken his self-esteem. His want of passion is horrible. Love of power he has. The fact that he is not deaf to public opinion makes him dangerous when affronted. Dull in many ways, he does not understand love. He is a master in the manipulation of others, but he does not know their motives if these motives are in the realm of the ideal. Coleridge spoke of Iago's casuistry as "the motive hunting a motiveless malignity." That fine phrase has almost wrecked the dramatic interpretation of Iago.

We know there are persons who get a certain satisfaction out of torturing people who are in their power; we call them sadists. But Iago is not like that. In the sixteenth century as well as today there was a relentless struggle for survival. Shakespeare must have been aware of this struggle and must have known participants in it. He may have seen persons ruined by ambition or made ruthless by disappointment or injustice. Iago is no stranger than is any such man. Disappointment over military promotion may well have started him on his cruel path. It is doubtful if he ever dreamed of the real end of his efforts. Used to the gains to be made from the stupid Roderigo, Iago never in his wildest fancy caught sight of the ruin to be accomplished by the innocence of Desdemona. Good women, ignorant and innocent of the world, may, in certain circumstances, be like dynamite. It is because evil makes tools of such as they that its sinister power awes us. Evil also uses incapable people in high places, like Othello, makes them commit blunders, which in turn may be used to generate other evils. Thus horror piles on horror, and evil adds deed to deed.

With reference to Iago, it should also be added that he has a method perfectly appropriate to him and his calling and especially effective for the task he has before him. Iago is a master opportunist. Could such a man as Iago drive such a man as Othello into jealousy and murderous frenzy? Shakespeare thought that he could. . . .Perhaps the central, the greatest, quality of drama is dramatic suspense, and we find in this play one of the greatest achievements of that kind. Let us see how it operates, how a good man at the very acme of happiness and contentment may step by step be driven to the uttermost extreme of wretchedness. Let us remember also that in order to accomplish this, Shakespeare, before the trial begins, has thought it wise to shift his scene to Cyprus. These things could hardly have happened in Venice, where the unity of the action could not have been so intensified.

The first act of *Othello*, and to a certain extent every other part of the play, has a decidedly realistic quality. The first scene serves to characterize Iago as a professional soldier. He is sure of his own deserts. He is a practical soldier and has all the contempt of the veteran for Cassio, "that never set a squadron in the field" (Act I, Sc. 1, 26-7, 36-8).

> Mere prattle, without practice,
> Is all his soldiership. . . .

The command is to blame.

> 'Tis the curse of service,
> Perferment goes by letter and affection,
> And not by old gradation, where each second
> Stood heir to the first.

Iago has not only been wronged, he has been insulted. He is not a nobody; he has influence with the great ones of the city; but he has been non-suited. What is worse, Othello has evaded Iago's backers

"with a bombast circumstance horribly stuffed with epithets of war";
and, when it came to the soldier-to-soldier meeting, Othello has bluntly
said, "I have already chose my officer." By nature and long training
Iago does not admit any motive of an idealistic nature. Othello has seen
him in action "at Rhodes, at Cyprus, and on other grounds." Othello
simply has lost his own pride and purposes and has turned
his back on justice. A situation exists, Othello wedded to Desdemona
without her father's consent, and Iago goes to work on what he has.
Iago raises an outcry and shouts vulgarities in the street. What he does is
calculated to confirm the aristocratic Brabantio in his sense of disgrace.
Iago renders the marriage preposterous in the old man's eyes. With
reference to Iago's revelation of his hatred of Othello and of his
temporizing, opportunistic method, it may be noted that he usually
speaks truth to Roderigo. In the second scene Othello is summoned to
the senate house, and modern stage-craft has almost bettered
Shakespeare in delaying Othello's entry until line 59 in the second scene.
Salvini's

> Keep up your bright swords, for the dew will rust them

was said to be magnificent. The second and third scenes build Othello up
to a towering height. His description of his courtship is one of the most
winning speeches in all Shakespeare, although a tragic premonition lurks
in Brabantio's obduracy (Act I, Sc. 3, 193-8, 293-4):

> I here do give thee that with all my heart
> Which, but thou hast already, with all my heart
> I would keep from thee. . . .
> Look to her, Moor, if thou hast eyes to see:
> She has deceived her father, and may thee.

At line 260 one notes that Desdemona wishes to accompany Othello
to Cyprus, a desire which is set down to her as a fault in Cinthio's story.
A fair interpretation of the long and twisted interview between Iago and
his dupe would be to see in it, in addition to Iago's skill in manipulating
Roderigo to his purpose, certain qualities in Iago. He is not only cynical
but wrong-headed. He actually does not know the higher nature in man
or woman. After he has given his convincing picture of the doctrine of
self-seeking, beginning "Our bodies are our gardens," he goes on to tell
Roderigo that it "cannot be that Desdemona should long continue her
love to the Moor."

> If sanctimony and a frail vow betwixt an erring barbarian and
> a super-subtle Venetian be not too hard for my wits and all the
> tribe of hell, thou shalt enjoy her.

"I cannot believe that in her; she's full of most blessed condition,"
says Roderigo in a later similar scene (Act II, Sc. 1, 254-8). "Blessed
fig's-end!" says Iago, "The wine she drinks is made of grapes: if she had
been blessed, she would never have loved the Moor." It is natural to
think that these things are only lies told to deceive Roderigo, but the

matter is not so simple as that. Iago actually does not comprehend virtue or believe in its existence. How else explain the later soliloquy (Act II, Sc. 1, 280-1):

> That Cassio loves her, I do well believe it;
> That she loves him, 'tis apt and of great credit.

He is very primitive in his knowledge of people, knows behavior not character. He knows that (Act I, Sc. 3, 405-8)

> The Moor is of a free and open nature,
> That thinks men honest that but seem to be so,
> And will as tenderly be led by the nose
> As asses are.

He knows that because he has tried it out, but he suspects Othello and Emilia of incontinency and does not know in any honest inferential judgment that his suspicions are groundless. Iago's final soliloquies in both Act I, Scene 3, and Act II, Scene 1, are very perfect in their depiction of the opportunist attitude. One sees him poised and waiting, ready to strike when opportunity offers. It is indeed very doubtful whether Othello did not make a great mistake in not placing this perfect tactician ·in high military command. As a strategist he is nothing; his plots are at once vague and limited, but his actions are unerring.

In the third scene of the second act we draw nearer to the great action. We see Iago in the role of the good fellow, a role which for his own interests army life would have taught him. He skillfully contrives to have Cassio provoked to a drunken rage and in the midst of the brawl knowingly has the alarm sounded. He understands the methods of enraging a commanding officer, and his plan works. We see Othello's capacity for passion in his ominous speech (Act II, Sc. 3, 204-17).

> Now, by heaven,
> My blood begins my safer guides to rule;
> And passion, having my best judgement collied,
> Assays to lead the way: if I once stir,
> Or do but lift this arm, the best of you
> Shall sink in my rebuke. Give me to know
> How this foul rout began, who set it on;
> And he that is approved in this offence,
> Though he had twinn'd with me, both at a birth,
> Shall lose me. What! in a town of war,
> Yet wild, the people's hearts brimful of fear,
> To manage private and domestic quarrel,
> In night, and on the court and guard of safety!
> 'Tis monstrous.

With the end of the second act, Iago's wits quickened to rapid action, the arrangements for his deceit are complete. The great example of dramatic suspense, where one thought or one act grows naturally out of its predecessor, begins with the third scene. One will note that Iago's hands are bare. He has nothing but an evil intention; for, though he does bring in Othello "jump" when he may find Cassio soliciting Desdemona's aid, nothing seems to come of it. Iago sows his first little seed in the soil, "Ha! I like not that," and hears the tender Desdemona say,

> What! Michael Cassio,
> That came a-wooing with you, and so many a time.

But when Desdemona leaves the stage Othello marks his love, his faith, and his happiness:

> Excellent wretch! Perdition catch my soul,
> But I do love thee! And when I love thee not,
> Chaos is come again.

Starting from this high point of Othello's love and confidence, Iago betters him down by one stroke after another. One may count more than a score of varied attacks. Iago's main weapon is false interpretation (Act III, Sc. 3, 38-39):

> That he would steal away so guilty-like,
> Seeing you coming.

He makes use of what he has (95-6):

> Did Michael Cassio, when you woo'd my lady,
> Know of your love?

He uses also the direct provocation to inquiry (97-8):

> But for a satisfaction of my thought;
> No further harm.

He resorts to platitudes as bases for procedure and for provocation to further question (125):

> Men should be what they seem.

He establishes the state of mind he desires to create by declaring or inferring that it already exists (165-7):

> O, beware, my lord, of jealousy;
> It is the green-eyed monster which doth mock
> The meat it feeds on.

Or consider line 214:

> I see this hath a little dash'd your spirits.

He recommends delay and espial, not only an excellent method of villainy to prevent face-to-face settlement, but a course peculiarly difficult for Othello (247-50):

> For, sure, he fills it up with great ability,
> Yet, if you please to hold him off awhile,
> You shall by that perceive him and his means.

He reinforces his carefully established reputation for innocence and honesty, does not forget that it is the main base from which he operates (375-6):

> O wretched fool,
> That livest to make thine honesty a vice!

He works from within and cuts down Othello's will to resist (395-6):

> Would you, the supervisor, grossly gape on—
> Behold her topp'd?

In lines 413-26 he launches his first great palpable lie. He has prepared Othello to swallow it. All the way through, we must remember, his task has been easy. Hamlet would have torn Iago's stratagems to tatters; Othello cannot.

> In sleep I heard him say 'Sweet Desdemona,
> Let us be wary, let us hide our loves.'

Iago next resorts to a device provided for in the source (434-5):

> Have you not sometimes seen a handkerchief
> Spotted with strawberries in your wife's hand?

Iago has got possession of the handkerchief and by the agency of the loyal Emilia. She is doubtful about letting him have it, because she knows his villainous practices, but he snatches it and gives her no satisfaction. As to the stealing of it, it is a simple matter. The Elizabethans were great pilferers. When Elizabeth was on her progresses and entertained at noblemen's houses, her entourage stole spoons and everything that they could lay their hands on from her hosts. The lie about the handkerchief's being in Cassio's possession produces what is perhaps the turning point of the tragedy. Othello is convinced and his passion is stirred. He himself knows its power (451-60).

From this time on Iago's task is confirmation; he has only to secure his case. In the presence of violent enactments of rage he shows an increasing uneasiness, as if he has let loose forces he does not know how to control. His activity still continues and he not only maintains in Othello a head of dangerous passion but, willingly or unwillingly, increases it. His greatest trial comes in the first scene of the fourth act when Othello demands that Iago shall make good his charges. The handkerchief then becomes the chief device by which Iago operates. Othello's description of it (Act III, Sc. 4, 55-75) elevates it into a mighty symbol, and Desdemona's lie makes of it a tragic instrument. Why did Desdemona lie? Why do the weak lie? And with the terrible Othello storming over her, is she more to blame than are the weak? The truth, to be sure, would have saved her, but paradoxically it is he and not she who kills the truth.

A fourth act normally shows the working out of the central action or motive of a tragedy, and the fourth act of *Othello* observes this principal in many interesting ways. It shows the depths to which Othello has already fallen in his degeneration. Iago can now be crude: there is no longer occasion for finesse. When the fourth act opens, Iago is conducting a pseudo-argument that to kiss in private is no matter,

> Or to be naked with her friend in bed.

Othello is not without some incredulity, but Iago's defence is as clever as his offence (Act IV, Sc. 1, 30-1):

> He [Cassio] hath, my lord; but be you well assured,
> No more than he'll unswear.

Lines 66-8 present the ancient insulting consolation for the cuckold:

> Good sir, be a man;
> Think every bearded fellow that's but yoked
> May draw with you.

The double scenes of this act are marvels of clever intrigue; for example, in lines 107-8;

> Now, if this suit lay in Bianca's power,
> How quickly should you speed!

Iago speaks to Cassio about Bianca, but leads Othello to believe he is speaking of Desdemona (167):

> Did you perceive how he laugh'd at his vice?

Here Iago says "his vice." Up to this point he has not directly maligned Desdemona; but, when he decides that she must go and go without a chance to speak, he lays blame on her (203-4):

> Do it not with poison, strangle her in her bed, even the bed
> she hath contaminated.

Observe that Othello calls Desdemona "whore" and "devil," and that this noble warrior strikes a woman.

There are other points of fourth-act interest. The second scene furnishes a perfect example of a moment of final suspense. Words are the deeds of drama, and Emilia is eloquent in defense of Desdemona. Incidentally her defense of women (Act IV, Sc. 3, 68-104) is a brilliant exaltation of the ordinary and a convincing evidence of Shakespeare's almost illimitable breadth of mind. It is perhaps a feature of a fourth act also that one should find a revelation of emotional tone, and in Desdemona's mention of her mother's maid called Barbara and her singing of the song of "Willow" our expectations are confirmed.

Shakespeare seems to have known that he was dealing with a tragic hero with his fatal pride. Othello assumes the rôle of eternal righteousness. Shakespeare could hardly have been unconscious of the thing he is having his hero do (Act V, Sc. 2, 1-22):

> It is the cause, it is the cause, my soul. . . .
> this sorrow's heavenly.

Later (294-5) he says of himself,

> An honourable murderer, if you will;
> For nought I did in hate, but all in honour.

Othello, like all such tragic heroes, suffers or is blessed with a revelation of himself to himself. He comes to himself too late. Iago has fooled him to the top of his bent and has built up in Othello such a fortress of passion that Othello rejects both his own better judgment and nature together with all normal testimony to the truth. He is deaf to the importunity of Desdemona herself. Nobody has ever known better than Shakespeare the passion of one who pleads for his life. Othello, taking on himself the justice of God, the acme of tragic madness in both ancient and modern drama, destroys Desdemona. Then the calm floods of a sane, objective world overwhelm him, and he sees what he has done. It is then that he says (Act V, Sc. 2, 259-81):

> Behold, I have a weapon;
> A better never did itself sustain
> Upon a soldier's thigh: I have seen the day,
> That, with this little arm and this good sword,
> I have made my way through more impediments
> Than twenty times your stop: but, O vain boast!
> Who can control his fate? 'tis not so now.
> Be not afraid, though you do see me weapon'd;
> Here is my journey's end, here is my butt,
> And very sea-mark of my utmost sail.
> Do you go back dismay'd? 'tis a lost fear;
> Man but a rush against Othello's breast,
> And he retires. Where should Othello go?
> Now, how dost thou look now? O ill-starr'd wench!
> Pale as thy smock! when we shall meet at compt,
> This look of thine will hurl my soul from heaven,
> And fiends will snatch at it. Cold, cold, my girl!
> Even like thy chastity. O cursed slave!
> Whip me, ye devils,
> From the possession of this heavenly sight!
> Blow me about in winds! roast me in sulphur!
> Wash me in steep-down gulfs of liquid fire!
> O Desdemona! Desdemona! dead!

From this and from his last great speech one knows that Othello has, as E.A. Robinson has it in his poem, looked into the eyes of Amaranth and seen himself as he is.

There is one other important question to be asked. Does Shakespeare in *Othello*, perhaps for the first time, develop the notion that, not a man's faults only, but his virtues may involve him in tragic consequences? He seems to do so, and it is a cruel idea, for it makes of human life a fearful thing. . . Perhaps Brutus's virtues caused him to mismanage the conspiracy and the war which his patriotism had led him to enter. It is perhaps nothing unusual for good men and women to be destroyed in literature and life because of their goodness, but the spectacle is always shocking. It would make this a perilous world if we should train ourselves in virtuous living only to find that our arduously acquired merits may themselves lead us into tragic error and tragic guilt. Of course this calamity often befalls minor and dependent characters in Shakespeare. Ophelia, in her gentle obedience to her father and brother, was an example of Elizabethan womanhood and is to this day an admirable and recognized type. Her very virtues prevent her from understanding and supporting Hamlet. Cordelia might be another case. Desdemona's sweetness and mercy help to bring about her own destruction. But here we have a hero, a man of impeccable justice, courage, and efficiency—virtues he needed in order to be a soldier and a leader of men—indeed, to be Othello—and yet that irresistible drive of passionate rectitude makes of him the victim of deceit and the architect of ruin.

By Hardın Craig, *An Interpretation of Shakespeare*, Lucas Brothers, 1948.

Selected Criticisms

The beauties of this play impress themselves so strongly upon the attention of the reader, that they can draw no aid from critical illustration. The fiery openness of *Othello*, magnanimous, artless, and credulous, boundless in his confidence, ardent in his affection, inflexible in his resolution, and obdurate in his revenge; the cool malignity of *Iago*, silent in his resentment, subtle in his designs, and studious at once of his interest and his vengenance; the soft simplicity of *Desdemona*, confident of merit, and conscious of innocence, her artless perseverance in her suit, and her slowness to suspect that she can be suspected, are such proofs of *Shakespeare's* skill in human nature, as, I suppose, it is vain to seek in any modern writer. The gradual progress which *Iago* makes in the Moor's conviction, and the circumstances which he employs to inflame him, are so artfully natural, that, though it will perhaps not be said of him as he says of himself, that he is *a man not easily jealous*, yet we cannot but pity him when at last we find him *perplexed in the extreme*.

There is always danger lest wickedness conjoined with abilities should steal upon esteem, though it misses of approbation; but the character of *Iago* is so conducted, that he is from the first scene to the last hated and despised.

Even the inferior characters of this play would be very conspicuous in any other piece, not only for their justness but their strength. *Cassio* is brave, benevolent, and honest, ruined only by his want of stubbornness to resist an insidious invitation. *Roderigo's* suspicious credulity, and impatient submission to the cheats which he sees practised upon him, and which by persuasion he suffers to be repeated, exhibit a strong picture of a weak mind betrayed by unlawful desires, to a false friend; and the virtue of Emilia is such as we often find, worn loosely, but not cast off, easy to commit small crimes, but quickened and alarmed at atrocious villainies.

The Scenes from the beginning to the end are busy, varied by happy interchanges, and regularly promoting the progression of the story; and the narrative in the end, though it tells but what is known already, yet is necessary to produce the death of *Othello*.

Had the scene opened in *Cyprus*, and the preceding incidents been occasionally related, there had been little wanting to a drama of the most exact and scrupulous regularity.

Samuel Johnson

The evil smell of sin is in *Othello* as constantly kept as before us as are its foulness and dirt. When Iago tentatively suggests to Othello that in choosing to marry him — a black man — Desdemona has already shown a perverted and unnatural taste, he exclaims:

> Foh! one may smell in such a will most rank,
> Foul disproportion, thoughts unnatural.

. . . and Othello brings out the horror of the contrast between the fair looks of Desdemona and what he believes her deeds entirely by means of smell, lamenting,

> O thou weed
> Who art so lovely fair and smell'st so sweet
> That the sense aches at thee, would thou hadst
> ne'er been born!

and answering her piteous query,

> Alas, what ignorant sin have I committed?

with the agonised cry,

> What committed!
> Heaven stops the nose at it.

. . .In *Othello* we see a low type of life, insects and reptiles, swarming and preying on each other, not out of special ferocity, but just in accordance with their natural instincts, mischievous and irresponsible wild cats, goats and monkeys, or the harmless, innocent animal trapped or beaten. This reflects and repeats the spectacle of the wanton torture of one human being by another, which we witness in the tragedy, the human spider and his fly. . . .

Caroline F.E. Spurgeon

Of all Shakespeare's tragedies, . . .not even excepting *King Lear*, *Othello* is the most painfully exciting and the most terrible. From the moment when the temptation of the hero begins, the reader's heart and mind are held in a vice, experiencing the extremes of pity and fear, sympathy and repulsion, sickening hope and dreadful expectation. . . .

Let me first set aside a mistaken view. I do not mean the ridiculous notion that Othello was jealous by temperament, but the idea, which has some little plausibility, that the play is primarily a study of a noble barbarian, who has become a Christian and has imbibed some of the civilisation of his employers, but who retains beneath the surface the savage passions of his Moorish blood and also the suspiciousness regarding female chastity common among Oriental peoples, and that the last three Acts depict the outburst of these original feelings through the thin crust of Venetian culture. . . . I do not mean that Othello's race is a matter of no account . . . But in regard to the essentials of his character it is not important . . .

This character is so noble, . . . and his sufferings are so heart-rending, that he stirs . . . in most readers a passion of mingled love and pity which they feel for no other hero in Shakespeare . . . Yet there are some critics . . . who cherish a grudge against him. They do not merely think that in the later stages of his temptation he showed a certain obtuseness, and that, to speak pedantically, he acted with unjustifiable precipitance and violence; no one, I suppose, denies that. But, even when they admit that he was not of a jealous temper, they consider that he *was* "easily jealous"; they seem to think that it was inexcusable in him to feel any suspicion of his wife at all; and they blame him for never suspecting Iago or asking him for evidence . . .

Othello . . . was trustful, and thorough in his trust. He put entire confidence in the honesty of Iago, who had not only been his companion in arms, but, as he believed, had just proved his faithfulness in the matter of the marriage. This confidence was misplaced, and we happen to know it; but it was no sign of stupidity in Othello. For his opinion of Iago was the opinion of practically everyone who knew him: and that opinion was that Iago was before all things "honest,". . .

Iago does not bring these warnings to a husband who had lived with a wife for months and years and knew her like his sister or his bosom-friend . . . But he was newly married; in the circumstances he cannot have known much of Desdemona before his marriage; . . .

. . . In Othello's case, after a long and most artful preparation, there now come . . . the suggestions that he is not an Italian, nor even a European; that he is totally ignorant of the thoughts and the customary morality of Venetian women; that he had himself seen in Desdemona's deception of her father how perfect an actress she could be. As he listens in horror, for a moment at least the past is revealed to him in a new and dreadful light, and the ground seems to sink under his feet. These suggestions are followed by a tentative but hideous and humiliating insinuation of what his honest and much-experienced friend fears may be the true explanation of Desdemona's rejection of acceptable suitors, and of her strange, and naturally temporary, preference for a black man. . . .

Now I repeat that *any* man situated as Othello was would have been disturbed by Iago's communications, and I add that many men would have been made wildly jealous.

A.C. Bradley

. . . As all within *Othello* — save the Iago-theme — is separated, differentiated, solidified, so the play itself seems at first to be divorced from wider issues, a lone thing of meaningless beauty in the Shakespearian universe, solitary, separate, unyielding and chaste as the moon. It is unapproachable, yields itself to no easy mating with our minds. Its thought does not readily mesh with our thought. We can visualize it, admire its concrete felicities of phrase and image, the mosaic of its language, the sculptural outline of its effects, the precision and chastity of its form. But one cannot be lost in it, subdued to it, enveloped by it, as one is drenched and refreshed by the elemental cataracts of *King Lear*; one cannot be intoxicated by it as by the rich wine of *Antony and Cleopatra*. *Othello* is essentially outside us, beautiful with a lustrous, planetary beauty. Yet the Iago-conception is of a different kind from the rest of the play. This conception alone, if no other reason existed, would point the necessity of an intellectual interpretation. So we see the Iago-spirit gnawing at the root of all the *Othello* values, the *Othello* beauties; he eats into the core and heart of this romantic world, worms his way into its solidity, rotting it, poisoning it. Once this is clear, the whole play begins to have meaning. On the plane of dramatic humanity, we see a story of the cynic intriguing to ruin the soldier and his love. On the plane of poetic conception, in matters of technique, style, personification — there we see a spirit of negation, colourless, and undefined, attempting to make chaos of a world of stately, architectural, and exquisitely coloured forms . . . Thus the different technique of the Othello and Iago conceptions is intrinsic with the plot of the play: in them we have the spirit of negation set against the spirit of creation. That is why Iago is undefined, devisualized, inhuman, in a play of consummate skill in concrete imagery and vivid delineation. He is a colourless and ugly thing in a world of colour and harmony. His failure lies in this: in the final scene, at the moment of his complete triumph, Emilia dies for her mistress to the words of Desdemona's willow-song, and the *Othello* music itself sounds with a nobler cadence, a richer flood of harmonies, a more selfless and universalized flight of the imagination than before. The beauties of the *Othello* world are not finally disintegrated: they make "a swan-like end, fading in music."

G. Wilson Knight

In short, it seems to me that by means of Iago's soliloquies; by means of character contrast with the brutally clear-eyed Iago, the earthy Emilia, the self-honest Cassio (who, also, be it remembered, openly admits his relationship to Bianca); by means of action contrast in the rejoinders of Roderigo, Cassio and Emilia to the proposal that Desdemona is unchaste; by means of Othello's own words in the first and second acts; by means of a carefully drawn Othello in the temptation scene who considers himself much stronger than he actually is; by means of sundry touches throughout which show Othello refusing to recognize

125

his own passionate nature; by means of a broken Othello in the last act, who tries to hang on to his nobility by refusing to face the fact of his murder — by means of all this Shakespeare has shown us that his hero is not as strong or as good a man as he thinks he is, that the hero's flaw is his refusal to face the reality of his own nature. This Othello, who (I think) is the Othello Shakespeare intended to convey, is rather different from the modern Othello, who is always thoroughly noble—before, during, and after his downfall . . .

The Othello that Shakespeare presents is nobly tragic in the same sense in which Macbeth and Anthony and Coriolanus and Lear are nobly tragic. Shakespeare's tragic protagonist is noble, but he is not altogether noble. He represents Aristotle's dictum:

> A man not preeminently virtuous and just, whose misfortune, however, is brought upon him not by vice or depravity but by some error of judgment, he being one of those who enjoy great reputation and prosperity . . . The change in the hero's fortunes must be . . . from happiness to misery; and the cause of it must lie not in any depravity, but in some great error on his part; the man himself being either such as we have described, or better, not worse, than that. (*Poetics*, Chapter 13)

It is not the hero's nobility in Shakespeare's tragedies but the flaw, the sin or error that all flesh is heir to, that destroys him. It is the close interweaving of great man, mere man, and base man that makes of Othello the peculiarly powerful and mysterious figure he is. In him Shakespeare shows the possible greatness, the possible baseness not only closely allied in what is after all mere man but also so casually connected that one must perforce wonder and weep.

Leo Kirschbaum

We could take it. . .that this opening view of Iago, the first impression he is to make, was meant to be the true one, if only because Shakespeare, in first presenting a character, never deliberately misleads us, is accustomed, rather, to sketch in its chief features, then and there, as unmistakably as possible, so as to leave us in no doubt from the start as to the sort of man or woman this is. . . .And here, in the first two scenes, in the contrast between the men, and in the boasted hate and its masking, are the main factors of the play already defined and set in motion. . . .With Macbeth, with Antony, amid the clashes of *King Lear*, the destructive force is one of the nobler human ardours turned to evil and the battle-ground — as so notably with Hamlet — is the hero's soul. Here the evil impulse is externalized in Iago; and if Othello's soul be a battle-ground, he himself puts up no fight on it. Nor can the jealousy which undoes him be properly called a degrading of the love it supplants; it is an aberration rather, a craze, and an ignoble one. Iago innoculates him with it, as with a disease, and after the feeblest of struggles — he is lost. *Othello* is not, therefore, a spiritual tragedy in the sense that the others may be called so. It is only the more painful for that; an all but intolerable exhibition, indeed, of human wickedness and folly, which does not so much purge us with pity and terror as fill us with horror and with anger that such a shoddy creature as Iago, possessed by his mountebank egoism, his envy and spite, should be able unresisted to destroy an Othello and bring Desdemona to her death. This incongruity is the keynote of the tragedy, and Shakespeare, therefore, strikes it clearly to begin with. And the actor who tries, here or later, to present Iago as a sort of half-brother to Milton's Satan falsifies both character and play. . . .

[Iago] is a passionless creature. Cinthio gives his wicked Ensign some motive for evil doing in jealousy, and a love for Desdemona ignored and so "changed into the bitterest hate." But Shakespeare admits neither love nor lust into Iago's composition, nothing so human; shows him to us, on the contrary, frigidly speculating upon the use such indulgence might be to him, and as frigidly deciding: none. Even his hate is cold, and will be the more tenacious for that, its strength not being spent in emotional ebb and flow. His endeavours then to respond suitably to Othello's outbursts—the flamboyant "Take note, take note, O world . . ." and the kneeling to echo and mock the oath by "yond marble heaven"—are simply histrionic, and overdone at that. And this, made plain to us, might be plain to Othello, were he not "eaten up with passion." For of intellectual excitement Iago *is* capable, and, elated by swift success, he begins to run risks. That stirs his cold blood; it is all that does.

Harley Granville-Barker

. . . The role of Desdemona is one of the most remarkable in Shakespeare. No woman in the plays is more pure than she, none whose every word is so compounded to kindliness, purity, and faith; and yet the aura of suspicion surrounding her is not purely of Iago's creation. Desdemona has married a Moor. About Othello's physical qualities we are left in no doubt. He is called "thick-lips" and "an old black ram." Elsewhere in Shakespeare, a black skin is viewed as revolting or as a symbol of evil . . . Shakespeare retained the black skin of Cinthio's character and added a further disabling feature—middle-age. In his own words, Othello is declined "into a vale of years." In the popular mind of Shakespeare's time as of today the attraction of an Othello for a Desdemona would have only one explanation—the waywardness of lust; Hamlet's most virulent attack upon his mother is informed with suspicion and disgust provoked by the ugliness of Claudius. Another suspicion attaching to Desdemona at the outset arises from the deception she has practiced upon her father. All Shakespeare's maidens in love deceive their fathers (except Ophelia), but only Desdemona's is permitted to speak as Brabantio speaks,

> Look to her, Moor, if thou hast eyes to see.
> She has deceiv'd her father, and may thee.

We may say that the speech serves to sow a seed in Othello's mind, but it also sows one in ours. Cinthio tells us directly that in marrying a Moor the lady was "not drawn by female appetite." Shakespeare makes no such apology. Instead Iago is permitted to harp upon the theme with terrible vividness:

> Foh! one may smell in such a will most rank,
> Foul disproportion, thoughts unnatural—

Shakespeare counters both Iago's charges and our predisposition in the matter by changing the Moor from the stealthy assassin he is in Cinthio to a man a pure woman might love, and by elevating Desdemona to the point of idealization.

Alfred Harbage

There is . . . a significant separateness of "worlds" in *Othello*; it is the separateness of Othello's world from that to which all the other characters equally belong. . . .Iago's world is the world of Venice, to which all the Venetians were born and in which they were imagined. It is more than that. It is society as Shakespeare now presented it. The central recommendation of society, so conceived, is cynically summed up in Iago's "Put money in thy purse." It is a world in which soldiers compete for office and prestige. It is a world in which, as Emilia well knows, men will do each other's offices in the women's beds. It is a world in which lust flaunts its finery and is not abashed. It is a world, indeed, from which spirit has been drained, and all is measured by use and entertainment and position. It is a kingdom of means, not ends.

We do not judge this society by any standard to which an actual society might attain. We do not set against it an ideal society towards which an actual society might asymptotically move. In judging the soceity of this Venice, we make a judgment on the very nature of all society whatsoever. We see that this society is, in fact, representative of society in general; and that society in general sets up use against value, expediency against integrity, prestige against principle, behaviour against moral being. In *Othello*, two worlds are set in opposition; the world set in time and inhabited by the Venetians; the world of the spirit, in terms of which we apprehend Othello. For this reason, in the bulk of the play, these Venetians are seen from the outside, they are seen as they behave; whereas Othello is seen from within, he is seen as he is.

Arthur Sewell

Othello is of great potential virtue, but when he comes upon the scene he is, like the early Hamlet, as yet untried. In spite of his age he has not yet encountered the evil of the world. The play will be his baptism; he will encounter evil as Adam had encountered it, and like Adam he will fall, but in his own destruction he will learn the nature of evil. He will learn to distinguish true virtue from seeming virtue, and from his tragedy he will emerge the kind of man who is capable of salvation. Shakespeare says in the destruction of Othello, as in that of

Hamlet, that true virtue and wisdom may come to man only through suffering, struggle and self-mastery. It is the tragedy of human life that this must be so.

. . . In *Othello* evil is an active force embodied in Iago. He is a dramatic symbol of evil whose function is to cause the downfall of Othello, and although Shakespeare endows him with an illusion of reality so supreme in its artistry that it has escaped analysis as thoroughly as that of Hamlet, in the larger symbolic design of the play he needs no specific motivation . . .

Desdemona is endowed, like Othello and Iago, with the illusion of reality, but in the total scheme of the play she stands from first to last as an incarnation of self-sacrificing love. She is a reflection of Christ, who must die at the hands of man, but out of whose death may spring man's redemption . . .

. . . The evil of her murder she will repay with foregiveness and mercy, out of evil creating good. Her unconquerable love for Othello will be his redemption.

Thus, although Othello dies accepting damnation as his just desert, Shakespeare by his careful delineation of Desdemona as a symbol of mercy has prepared the audience for the salvation of Othello in spite of all. Othello dies truly penitent. He takes the step which Claudius, in spite of his fears of damnation, cannot take. Othello destroys himself in an act of expiation, and his final words are a reminder to the audience of his union in death with the goodness he had tried to destroy:

> I kiss'd thee ere I killed thee: no way but this;
> Killing myself, to die upon a kiss.   (Act V, Sc. 2, 358-359)

The audience knows that in his renunciation of evil, his penance and expiation, Othello has merited salvation . . .

The tragedy of *Othello*, in its neatness and precision of construction, parallels more closely than any of Shakespeare's other plays what may be called the prototype of tragedy in Christian Europe, that of Adam in the garden of Eden. *Othello* expresses more perfectly than any of the other plays the paradox of the fortunate fall through which the Christian world could postulate a merciful and purposive God in spite of Adam's tragedy. The play is Christian in its symbolism and in the central intellectual proposition which shapes and controls the action, character and poetry of which it is comprised. *Othello* couches its universal propositions in terms of specific action and specific character, which in the speedy movement of the scenes retain an illusion of reality in spite of the logical inconsistencies which the scholar's study may reveal. It creates an emotional equivalent for its central idea and a tension between emotion and intellect which is the essence of tragedy. We participate fully in the horror which falls upon Othello, while rationally we are assured and seconded in our faith in divine order.

Irving Ribner

Bibliography

Bradley, A.C. *Shakespearean Tragedy*. London: The Macmillan Company, 1904; reprinted by World Publishing Co., Meridian Books, 1955.

Bryant, J.A. *"Othello,"* in *Hippolyta's View: Some Christian Aspects of Shakespeare's Plays*. Lexington, Kentucky: University of Kentucky Press, 1961.

Campbell, Lily B. *"Othello:* A Tragedy of Jealousy," in *Shakespeare's Tragic Heroes*. Cambridge, England: Cambridge University Press, 1930; reprinted by Barnes & Noble, Inc., 1960.

Charlton, H.B. *Shakespearian Tragedy*. Cambridge, England: Cambridge University Press, 1948.

Clemen, Wolfgang. *"Othello,"* in *The Development of Shakespeare's Imagery*. Cambridge, Mass.: Harvard University Press, 1951; reprinted by Hill and Wang.

Coleridge, Samuel Taylor. *Notes and Lectures Upon Shakespeare and Some Old Poets and Dramatists*. Vol. I. London: William Pickering, 1849.

Cunningham, J.V. "Reason Panders Will," *Woe or Wonder: The Emotional Effect of Elizabethan Tragedy*. Denver: Alan Swallow, 1951.

Eliot, T.S. "Shakespeare and the Stoicism of Seneca," *Selected Essays of T. S. Eliot*. 3rd rev. ed. London: Faber and Faber, Ltd., 1951.

Elliott, G.R., *The Flaming Minister*. Durham, North Carolina: Duke University Press, 1953.

Flatter, Richard. *The Moor of Venice*. London, 1950.

Gerard, Albert. " 'Egregiously An Ass': The Dark Side of the Moor. A View of Othello's Mind," *Shakespeare Survey,* 10 (1957); pp. 99-100.

Granville-Barker, Harley. *Prefaces to Shakespeare,* 4th series: *Othello*. London: Sidgewick and Jackson, Ltd., 1945.

Harbage, Alfred. *As They Liked It*. New York: The Macmillan Company, 1947; reprinted by Harper and Row, Torchbooks.

Hazlitt, William. *The Round Table* and *Characters of Shakespeare's Plays*. New York: E. P. Dutton, 1944.

Heilman, Robert B. *Magic In the Web*. Lexington, Kentucky: University of Kentucky Press, 1956.

Johnson, Samuel. *Johnson On Shakespeare,* ed. Walter Raleigh. London: Oxford University Press, 1908; reprinted 1949.

Kirschbaum, Leo. "The Modern Othello," *ELH, A Journal of English Literary History,* XI (1944). pp. 283-296.

Kittredge, George Lyman, ed. *The Complete Works of Shakespeare.* New York: Ginn and Co., 1936.

Knight, G. Wilson. *The Wheel of Fire.* Oxford University Press, 1930; Barnes and Noble, Inc., 1964.

Leavis, F.R. *The Common Pursuit.* Harmondsworth, Middlesex: Penguin Books, Ltd., 1963.

Muir, K. and Schoenbaum, S. *A New Companion to Shakespeare Studies.* Cambridge University Press, 1971.

Ribner, Irving. *Patterns In Shakespearian Tragedy.* New York: Barnes and Noble, Inc. 1960.

Rymer, Thomas. "A Short View of Tragedy," in *The Critical Works of Thomas Rymer,* ed. Curt A. Zimansky. New Haven: Yale University Press, 1956.

Rosenberg, Marvin. *The Masks of Othello.* Berkeley and Los Angeles: University of California Press, 1961.

Sewell, Arthur. *Character and Society in Shakespeare.* Oxford: Clarendon Press, 1951.

Siegel, Paul N. *"Othello," Shakespearean Tragedy and the Elizabethan Compromise.* New York: New York University Press, 1957.

Spivack, Bernard. *Shakespeare and the Allegory of Evil.* New York: Columbia University Press, 1958.

Sprague, Arthur Colby. *"Othello," Shakespeare and the Actors.* Cambridge, Mass.: Harvard University Press, 1944.

Spurgeon, Caroline F.E. *Shakespeare's Imagery.* New York: The Macmillan Company, 1935.

Stirling, Brents. "Reputation, Reputation, Reputation," *Unity in Shakespearian Tragedy.* New York: Columbia University Press, 1956.

Wilson, Harold S. *"Othello,"* On the Design of Shakespearian *Tragedy.* Toronto: University of Toronto Press, 1957.

NOTES

NOTES

NOTES